£14.99

HEINEMANN SKILLS

Business Presentations LEVEL 2

for the OCR Certificate in Text Processing

Sharon Spencer

Heinemann

Heinemann Educational Publishers,
Halley Court, Jordan Hill, Oxford OX2 8EJ
Part of Harcourt Education

Heinemann is a registered trademark of Harcourt Education Limited

First published 2003

07 06 05 04 03
10 9 8 7 6 5 4 3 2 1

British Library Cataloguing in Publication Data is available from British Library on request.

ISBN 0 435 45404 8

Typeset by J&L Composition, Filey, North Yorkshire

Printed in the UK by Thomson Litho Ltd

Cover design by Wooden Ark

Cover photo: © Gareth Boden

Acknowledgements
I would like to thank my family for their support while writing this book.
Sharon Spencer

The publishers would also like to thank Rosemary Wyatt at Abingdon College.

Screen shots reprinted with permission from Microsoft Corporation.

Every effort has been made to contact copyright holders of material reproduced in this book. Any ommissions will be rectified in subsequent printings if notice is given to the publishers.

Tel: 01865 888058
www.heinemann.co.uk

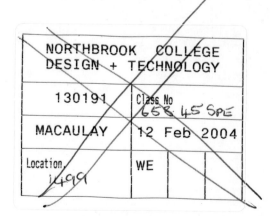

Contents

Introduction

Presentations – what are they?

A presentation is a series of slides which, when shown together, forms a complete presentation. You may have seen PowerPoint presentations at college or in the workplace. Often exhibitions and events have a PowerPoint presentation running on a computer screen or a large computerised projection screen. The slides move effortlessly from one to another giving a professional look.

The examination requires you to create a series of slides which, when shown together, form a complete presentation. Each of the slides will be printed so that the examiner can mark the hard copy. You will not be required to send in the presentation on a disk.

If you were using PowerPoint to prepare a presentation to use at work or at college, you would not necessarily need to print the 'slides'. You would use a computer screen or computerised projection screen to display the work directly to your audience. You may of course wish to print out handouts for the audience and this is covered in the book.

Although the OCR examination does not cover these aspects, you may also set your presentation to have animated effects and sound and to be timed so that the slides move from one to another at a precise time. Once you have covered the work needed for the examination it would be a good idea to practise using techniques such as adding animated effects and timing so that if you are called upon to create a presentation you will be able to create a professional image.

About the exam

The OCR Business Presentations Examinations Level 2 forms part of the OCR Text Processing Modular Awards suite of qualifications. The main aims are to:

- develop skill in the use of presentation software;
- develop the ability to produce a variety of routine and specialist presentations from hand-written and typewritten drafts and recalled presentations to a standard that would be acceptable in the workplace;
- encourage the development of practical skills that would be of benefit in workplace situations; and
- assist in the development of skills which would contribute to the achievement of the Key Skills in ICT at level 2.

The examination takes the form of a 1½-hour test which is set and marked by OCR Examinations Board. You will be expected to complete four tasks within the given time.

This examination is all about displaying information in a format that can be used at a presentation. This means that the speaker will have access either to an overhead projector or to computerised equipment. If using an overhead projector then the documents will be printed on to transparencies. If using computerised equipment then the information will be displayed in the form of a 'slide show'. The presenter will either click a remote control or press a key on the keyboard to move from slide to slide. It is possible for the slides to change automatically, timed on the computer. However, if a presenter is speaking then it is probably best to change the slides manually so that he or she can answer questions, etc.

The examination tests the skills necessary to make an effective presentation. The candidate is required to print out the documents created so that they can be marked. However, at the end of the examination a series of slides will have been created that, put together, would form the basis of a short talk.

About this book

The aim of this book is to provide a step-by-step guide to producing each of the documents required for the examination using PowerPoint. The main features are:

- A step-by-step guide to using PowerPoint to create each of the four examination tasks.
- Consolidation practice for each task to ensure you have thoroughly learned and understood the instructions.
- Examination practice to ensure that you are thoroughly prepared for the examination tasks.
- A useful section on common errors and how to resolve them.
- Worked examples of the exercises contained in the book.

Getting you started

Loading PowerPoint

To open PowerPoint you will need to be in Windows. How you load Windows will depend on whether you are using a networked or stand-alone system.

Exercise 1

1   Find out whether you are using a networked or stand-alone system.
2   Find out how to load Windows on your system.
3   Load Windows.

Once you have loaded Windows you will see the 'desktop'. This is the main menu from which you move around in Windows. It will look something like Figure 1, but the icons may differ according to the programs installed and the setup options that have been defined.

Figure 1 Windows Desktop

Once you have reached the desktop you will be ready to open PowerPoint. You may see a shortcut icon on the desktop which will take you straight to the PowerPoint software. If the icon is not on the desktop then you will need to open PowerPoint from the Program menu using the Start button.

Exercise 2

Method 1

1 Move the mouse cursor over the **Start** button and click the left mouse button – a pop-up menu will appear listing the various programs and applications installed on the computer.
2 Highlight **Programs** by moving the mouse over it – another menu will appear (see Figure 2).

Figure 2 Loading PowerPoint using the Start button

3 **Drag** the mouse across to **Microsoft PowerPoint** and click on it. PowerPoint will now begin to load.

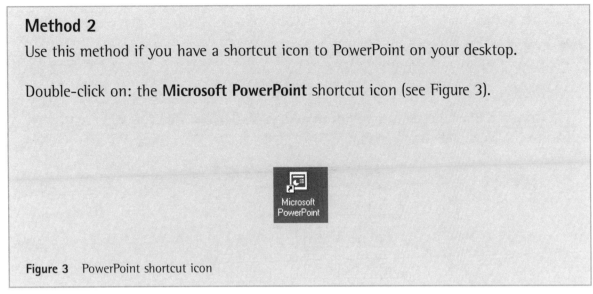

Method 2

Use this method if you have a shortcut icon to PowerPoint on your desktop.

Double-click on: the **Microsoft PowerPoint** shortcut icon (see Figure 3).

Figure 3 PowerPoint shortcut icon

Once PowerPoint has finished loading you will see the option box shown in Figure 4 on screen. If this does not appear then you will be taken straight to the **Choose Slide** option box.

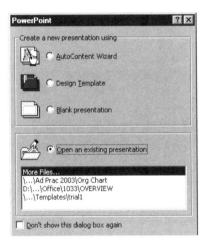

Figure 4 Microsoft PowerPoint option box

This catalogue gives you a choice of using ready-prepared designs (known as wizards), ready-prepared templates on which to base your presentation or a blank presentation. In this book you will learn how to set up blank presentations.

Choosing a presentation

As you will be setting up each slide individually you will need to choose a blank presentation. This means that you will place each piece of text, image or graph exactly where it is required. PowerPoint has a number of presentation wizards which, if chosen, will take you through, step by step, to a completed presentation. Your input would consist of keying in the correct text. The design elements, such as colours, borders and images, have already been chosen for you. Wizards can be useful if you are in a hurry. However, the OCR Business Presentations examination cannot be set up using a PowerPoint wizard. This means that you will need to create the presentation from scratch, adding all your own design elements.

Exercise 3

Create a blank presentation.

Method

Click on: the **Blank presentation** button and then click on: **OK.** This will then take you to the **New Slide box** (see Figure 5).

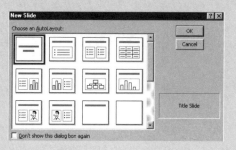

Figure 5   New Slide box

The 'slides' referred to in PowerPoint are really the pages of a document. The slide option gives a number of pages with text, graph and image frames set for you to fill in.

Exercise 4

Choose a slide option with placeholders (frames) for text and heading.

Method

1   Click on: the **Bulleted List** template. This will be highlighted by a blue frame. The words 'Bulleted List' will appear in the name box on the right-hand side of the dialogue box (see Figure 6).

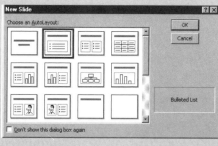

Figure 6   Bulleted list slide option highlighted

2   Click on: **OK.** A slide template will appear on screen (see Figure 7).

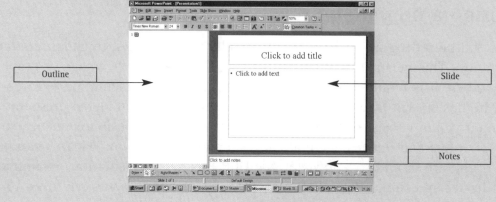

Figure 7   Bulleted list slide template

The view for this slide has been set as 'Normal' which is the default setting. We shall look at other views later on.

The screen consists of three 'panes' – that is, separate spaces in which to display the following:

Slide: The slide on which you are working will be displayed here.

Outline: This refers to the space on the left-hand side of the screen. It gives an overview of the entire presentation. As slides are added to the presentation the outline pane will be updated.

Notes: This allows you to input any notes that you want to make about the slide. We will be looking at this later in the book.

If you accidentally move to a different view, you can easily get back to the 'normal' view by doing one of the following.

Exercise 5

Move around the various view options.
Method
1   Go to the **View** menu on the toolbar.
2   If you are already in **Normal** view, choose: **Slide Sorter**; if not, click on: **Normal**
    or
3   Click on: the bottom left of the **Normal** icon on the **Slide Show View** bar which is displayed on the screen (see Figure 8).

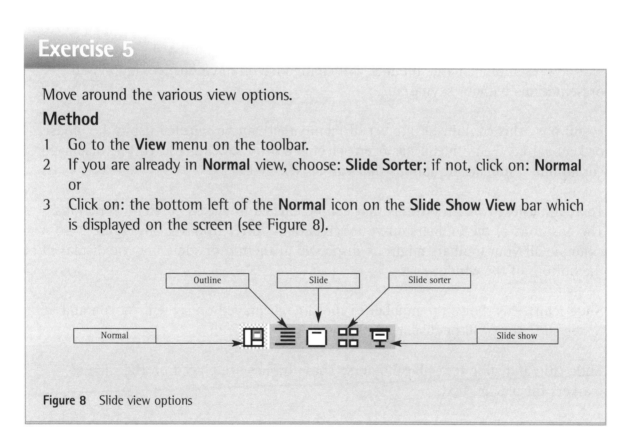

Figure 8   Slide view options

Toolbars and menus

Your window should now look similar to the one in Figure 9 – with a blank slide in the right-hand side. The toolbars (see below) may be in different positions.

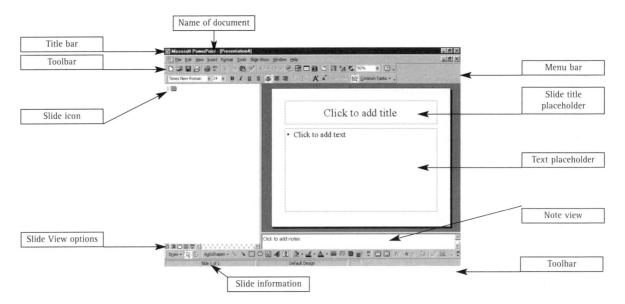

Figure 9   The Presentation window

Parts of the slide window

Title bar: This shows the name of the presentation and the application name (Microsoft PowerPoint). If you have not saved your presentation the name displayed will be Presentation 1 (the number will change if you have opened and closed presentations without saving).

Menu bar: This contains a number of menus that can be selected using the mouse or keyboard. When a menu has been selected a drop-down menu will be displayed containing a number of options that can be selected.

Toolbars: These contain buttons that can be clicked to access common functions. The positions of the toolbars on your screen may differ from that in Figure 9 – for example all your toolbars might be displayed at the top or some may be displayed at the bottom of the window.

Slide icon: This shows the number of the slide displayed on screen. As you add text to the slide so it will be displayed alongside the slide icon.

Slide title and **slide text placeholders:** These frames are placed on the slide as markers for placing text.

Slide View options: These buttons give shortcuts to the various views available.

Slide information: This tells you the number of the slide you have displayed and the number of slides contained in the presentation.

Note view: This space is where notes for the speaker can be added. As the text is keyed in so it will be displayed in this area.

Help menu

At some point you may need to access the various help options. To access the **Help** function, do the following.

Exercise 6

Access the **Help** function using various methods.

Method 1

Press the **F1** button at the top of the keyboard. The **Help** assistant will appear on screen. With the Answer Wizard tab selected, key in a question relating to the help you require.

Method 2

Click on: the **Help** button 🔃 on the toolbar.

Method 3

Click on: the **H**elp menu on the menu bar and select: Microsoft PowerPoint Help.

Undo/Redo

If you have made a mistake and wish to go back to where you were, you can use the Undo/Redo buttons which are situated on the toolbar (see Figure 10).

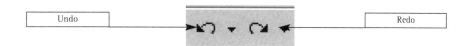

Figure 10   Undo and Redo buttons

The Undo button will remove the last action one by one to a maximum of 20. (The number of undo actions can be changed by choosing **O**ptions on the **T**ools menu – select the **Edit** tab and key in the number of undos in the box.)

The Redo button will redo an action that has been undone.

Saving a presentation

It is a good idea to save your work as often as possible. This will ensure that if anything goes wrong such as the computer crashing, your work will not be lost.

The first time you save a presentation you will need to give it a filename. After that you just need to save the work, usually without renaming it. However, for the examination you will need to print the slides after each set of changes and so it is a good idea to save under a different filename at each point where you are required to print the work. This will ensure that you do not overwrite your work and that all the slides are in place when you need to print.

Exercise 7

Save the presentation under the name **COLLEGE.**

Method

1   Go to **File** and choose: **Save As**. The menu as shown in Figure 11 will appear.

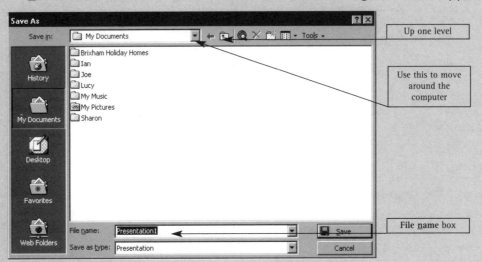

Figure 11   Save As menu

2   If the name of the folder in which you are going to save the work is on screen, then double-click on the name to open it.
3   If the name of the folder in which you are going to save the work is not on screen then you will need to find it. You can do this by clicking on the arrow alongside **My Documents** shown in Figure 11. This will show you the various components on the computer, such as the hard drive, a floppy drive (to take disks) or a CD-ROM drive. Click on the correct one and then using the same method move around to find the folder you want.
4   You may also use the **Up one level** icon which will move you around the existing folders and then the computer elements.
5   Once you have found and opened the correct folder, make sure the cursor is flashing in the **File name** box. Double-click in the filename box and key in the name of the presentation – in this exercise, **COLLEGE.**
6   Click on the **Save** box to save your work.

Exiting PowerPoint

Practise closing down and exiting PowerPoint.

Exercise 8

Close down and exit PowerPoint.

Method

1   Ensure you have saved your work using the method given above.
2   Go to **File** and choose: **Exit**. PowerPoint will now shut down safely.

Part 1

This part covers **Document 1** of the examination. This comprises the following:

- Creating a master slide.
- Setting the master slide styles.
- Creating four slides using the master slide.
- Printing individual slides and an outline view.

Creating a master slide

In this section you will learn how to:

- load PowerPoint and set up a master slide
- change the slide size
- apply a background
- insert a company name, the date and your name
- set slide numbering
- insert a company logo
- resize an image
- move an image.

The examination requires you to set up a master slide. That is a master page or template which contains elements such as a graphic, logo or text that will appear on each slide in the presentation. You only need to set a master page when you start creating your presentation. In order to do this you will need to move from the current screen to a 'master slide' screen on which these elements can be set.

Load PowerPoint

Exercise 1.1

Load PowerPoint and open the presentation you previously saved as filename **COLLEGE**.

Method

1 Load PowerPoint as instructed in the Introduction.
2 The PowerPoint sub-menu will appear. Choose: **Open an existing presentation** option. The existing presentations will be listed at the bottom of the menu (see Figure 1.1).
3 Choose the presentation you wish to open – in this case **COLLEGE**.
4 Click on: **OK**.

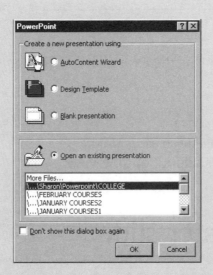

Figure 1.1   PowerPoint sub-menu

Note: If PowerPoint has already been loaded then do the following:

1   Go to **File.**
2   Go to **Open.**
3   A list of PowerPoint presentations should appear on screen. If the name of the presentation you wish to open is on screen, click on the name and then click on: **Open.**
4   If the name of your presentation does not appear, then check that you are in the correct directory. If you are not you will have to open the various folders until you find the correct one. To do this, use the **Name** box at the top of the page in the same way as was used for saving the file.

Set up a master slide

Exercise 1.2

Set up a master slide that can be used as the basis of the presentation.

Method

1   Go to the **View** menu on the toolbar.
2   Click on: **Master.** A new sub-menu will open.
3   Click on: **Slide Master.** A master slide template will appear on the screen (see Figure 1.2).

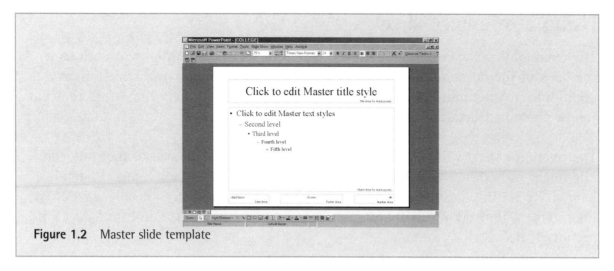

Figure 1.2   Master slide template

You will see that there are several placeholders already created on the master slide. These are the text frames you will use to enter text and graphic images.

Choosing a slide size

The default setting for slides in PowerPoint is **On-Screen Show** which means that the slides are sized for optimum viewing on a computerised screen. Obviously, this would normally be suitable for most purposes and would not need changing. However, as you are preparing the presentation to be printed on A4 paper for examination purposes it is better to change the slide size to A4 paper. When you do this the background covers most of the paper, except for the printer's margins, and the text and images are centred according to the size of the paper.

Change the slide size

Exercise 1.3

Change the slide size to A4 paper.

Method

1   Go to the **File** option on the menu bar.
2   Choose: **Page Setup**. The sub-menu as shown in Figure 1.3 will appear.

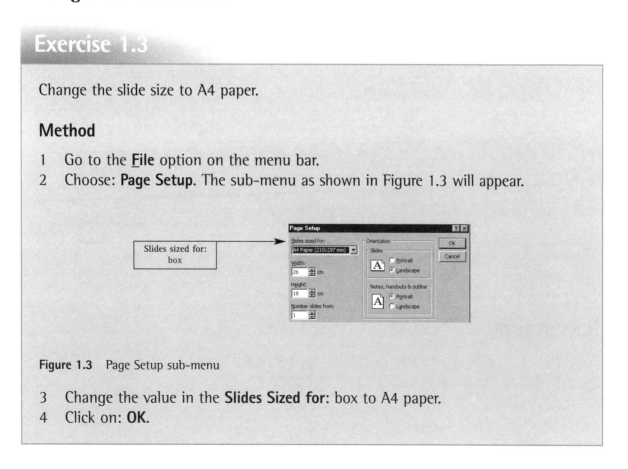

Figure 1.3   Page Setup sub-menu

3   Change the value in the **Slides Sized for:** box to A4 paper.
4   Click on: **OK**.

Using a reference sheet

The examination paper will give you instructions as to the contents of each slide. At the back of the question paper is a reference sheet (see Figure 1.4) which gives additional instructions regarding the house style. It is extremely important that you follow these instructions carefully as errors will be penalised.

The reference sheet will contain details such as the style and size of the font, the alignment of text and whether bullets are required (these are explained in detail below). By setting these requirements on the master slide, you will only have to set them once as PowerPoint will automatically use the correct size and font for each section of text.

REFERENCE SHEET

Follow the design brief, e.g. styles and layout within the ranges shown.

Design brief

Instructions for master slide style

The layout of the master slide text and graphics is not pre-defined but **must be** consistent across the slide show.

Component	Input	Additional information
Background	One used consistently throughout the presentation – software template or colour may be used	Ensure legibility of text against background on printout
Company name	NEW TOWN COLLEGE	Font: Default
Date	Today's date	Font: Default
Name	Insert your name	Font: Default
Slide numbering	Insert slide numbers	Font: Default
Company logo	Suitable graphic from Clip Art	Black and white or colour

---

Figure 1.4 Example of a style reference sheet

Background

This refers to a colour or pattern which appears in the background of each slide to make it visually more interesting. Look at Figure 1.5.

Figure 1.5   Master slide background

This textured background pattern gives some depth to the slide. However, you must be careful to ensure that the text and images which will be placed on the slides will be legible. It is therefore sensible to avoid dark colours or patterns.

Apply a background

Exercise 1.4

Apply a legible background to the master slide.

Method

1   Go to **Format** on the toolbar.
2   Click on: **Background**. The sub-menu shown in Figure 1.6 will appear.

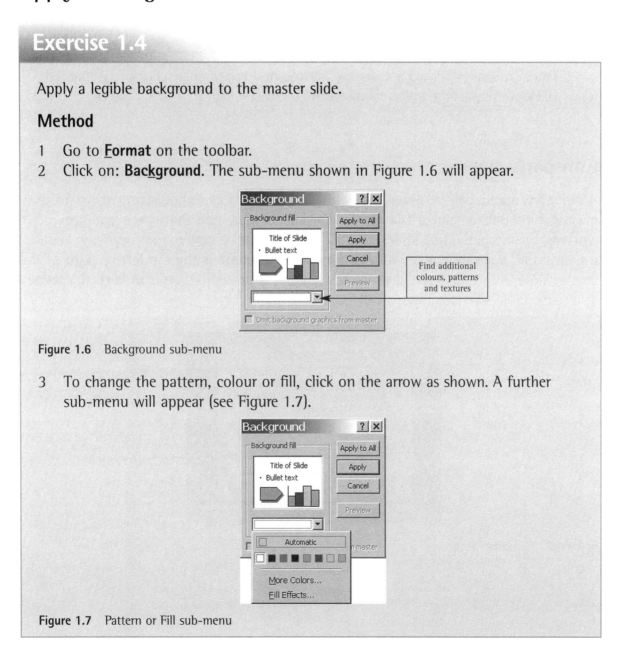

Figure 1.6   Background sub-menu

3   To change the pattern, colour or fill, click on the arrow as shown. A further sub-menu will appear (see Figure 1.7).

Figure 1.7   Pattern or Fill sub-menu

By clicking on **More colors** or **Fill Effects** you may change the appearance of the background. Figure 1.8 shows the different Fill effects you can use.

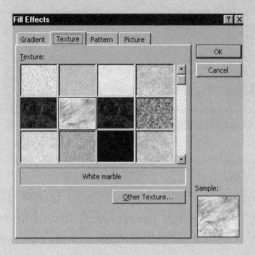

Figure 1.8   Fill Effects sub-menu

By clicking on the tabs at the top of the sub-menu you will be given a number of patterns, textures and gradients to choose from. Click on the one you would like to use and click on: **OK**.

4   Once you have finished setting the background appearance, click on: **Apply**. The background settings will be applied to the master slide.

Company name

A company name will be given for you to key in. This can appear anywhere on the master slide, but remember that this is the master slide and that when you are working on the individual slides, the text should not be covered in any way. With this in mind, a sensible place to add the company name is the top left or right of the master slide. In order to avoid problems later, it is probably better to keep the name at a reasonable size (see Figure 1.9).

Figure 1.9   Company name

Key in the company name

Key in the company name at the top left of the master slide so that it appears on each slide.

Method

1 Click on the text box icon . If the Drawing tools are not shown on screen, you will need to open them by going to **View**, choosing **Toolbars** and clicking on **Drawing**. The drawing tools will now be shown. Click on the text box icon.
2 Click at the top left-hand corner of the master slide and drag the text box out and down to form a text frame.
3 Click inside the text box in order to make the text cursor appear.
4 Key in: **NEW TOWN COLLEGE**.

Date

You will see from the reference sheet that today's date is required. This can be inserted in the date placeholder which is at the bottom left corner.

Insert the date

Insert the date in the date placeholder at the bottom of the master slide.

Method

1 Click in the <date/time> area of the placeholder.
2 Go to the **Insert** menu on the toolbar.
3 Click on: **Date and Time**. A date sub-menu will appear on screen (see Figure 1.10). You may choose the date display, but remember, the American display (month/day/year) is not acceptable for OCR examinations.

Figure 1.10 Date and Time sub-menu

> 4   Once you have chosen the correct date format for your slide, click on: **OK**. If you would like the date to be updated each time you open the slide presentation, then click in the **Update automatically** box.

Name

The second placeholder has a title 'footer area'. This means that the text you key in here will be repeated on every slide. Use this placeholder to insert your name.

Insert your name

Exercise 1.7

Insert your name in the centre placeholder at the bottom of the master slide.

Method

1   Click in the placeholder marked 'footer area'.
2   Key in your name using initial capitals (that is with a capital letter for the first letter of each word, lower case letters for the rest).

Slide numbering

This is just the same as page numbering. Once you have set the automatic slide numbering all your slides will be numbered. As the automatic slide numbering code has already been inserted into the master slide all you need to do is activate it.

Set slide numbering

Exercise 1.8

Activate the slide numbering facility in the bottom right-hand box of the master slide.

Method

1   Go to **View** on the menu bar.
2   Go to **Header and Footer**.
3   Ensure that the **Slide number** and **Footer** boxes are ticked (see Figure 1.11). (If they are not ticked they will not print.)
4   Click on: **Apply to All**.
5   Each slide should now be numbered, although you will not see the number until you close the master slide and return to Slide view.

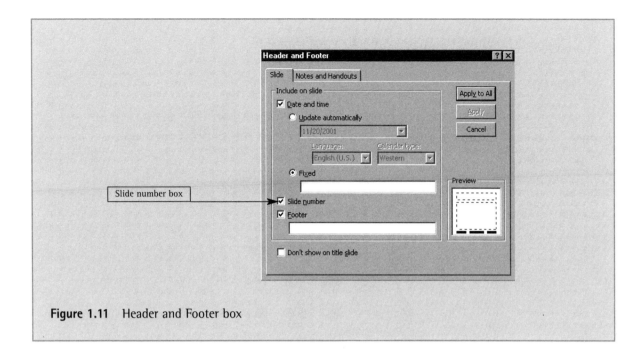

Figure 1.11   Header and Footer box

Company logo

The company logo for the purposes of the examination is just a piece of Clip Art (see below). You may choose any image. However, remember that, as it has to be printed on every page and must not touch any other text or image, it is better to keep the image quite small.

Insert the company logo

Exercise 1.9

Place an image to form the company logo at the top left-hand corner of the master slide.

Method

1   Go to **Insert** on the toolbar.
2   Click on: **Picture**. A sub-menu will appear (see Figure 1.12).

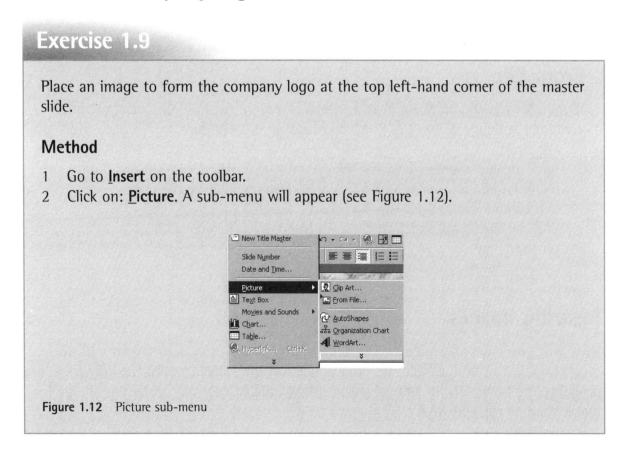

Figure 1.12   Picture sub-menu

3   Choose the correct source – **Clip Art** or **From File**.

Clip Art

If you are using Clip Art either from a disk or the hard disk drive of the computer then choose this option. You will then be taken into the Clip Art menu (see Figure 1.13).

Figure 1.13   Clip Art options

1   From this menu you can choose a category by clicking on one of the icons. Once you have chosen a category then Clip Art relating to that category will be displayed.
2   Choose an image by clicking on it. The Insert options will be displayed.
3   Choose the **Insert into Document** icon ▨ . The image will now be inserted into your document.
4   Click the **X** at the top right-hand corner to close the Clip Art screen.

Note: The image will appear in the centre of the slide in the default size. You will need to move and resize the image to fit in with the presentation.

From File

If you are choosing an image that has been stored on the hard disk drive of your computer, a floppy disk or CD-ROM, then choose this option:

1   Click on the From File icon ▨ From File... . You will be taken to an **Insert Picture** menu where you can view and choose a directory. Choose the correct directory and choose your image.
2   Click on the image and then click on: **Insert**. Your image will now be inserted on to the slide.

Resizing images

Now that you have an image on the slide you must position it so that it will not touch any text or images that are later placed on the slides. Again, the corners are probably the best place to start to position the image. You may resize the image to make it smaller if you wish.

Resize the image

Exercise 1.10

Resize the image so that it is approximately 3.5 cm high and 3.5 cm wide.

Method

1 **Right** click on the image to bring up a sub-menu.
2 Choose: **Format Picture**. The **Format Picture** sub-menu will appear.
3 Click on the **Size** tag at the top. The sub-menu will change to that shown in Figure 1.14.

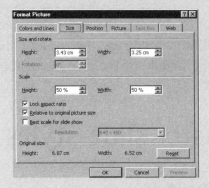

Figure 1.14   Format Picture menu

4 Enter the values into the **H<u>e</u>ight** and **Wi<u>d</u>th** boxes. If the **Lock <u>a</u>spect ratio** box is checked then you will only be able to enter one value – the other will change automatically so that the image remains in proportion. To remove the lock, take off the check box by clicking in it so that the tick disappears.
5 Click on: **OK**.

You will not be given a graphic size in the examination and so you may wish to resize the image manually rather than by accurate size.

Resize the image manually

Exercise 1.11

Method

1 Click on the image to select it. The handles of the image will be displayed.
2 Click on a **Corner** handle. It is important that you use a corner handle so that the image remains in proportion (see Figure 1.15).

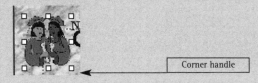

Corner handle

Figure 1.15   Clip Art handles

> 3 Drag the image diagonally so that it reduces in size. You should always use the corner handles so that the image is reduced proportionately. This means that the height and width will reduce at the same rate ensuring the image looks the same, just smaller.

Move the image

Method

Click on the image to select it. Keeping the mouse button held down, drag the image to the required position. Do not use the corner handles to do this as it will resize the image. Click in the middle of the image and then drag image to required position.

Setting the master slide styles

In this section you will learn how to:

- change the text font and size
- add emphasis
- change the alignment
- set the bullet and sub-bullet text styles
- adjust the space
- close and save the master slide.

Now you have added the items which need to be shown on each page you will need to set the master slide styles. The reference sheet (Figure 1.16) gives the settings for the font, point size, alignment and enhancement. You can set these on the master slide styles so that each time you key in a heading or bullet text the settings will be the same.

The examination will give a list of slides to be prepared together with instructions as to the text styles. The text styles to be used are given on the reference sheet at the back of the examination paper.

Style	Font	Size	Emphasis	Alignment
Heading	Sans-serif	44–60	Bold	Centre
Bullet	Sans-serif	28–34	Default	Left
Sub-bullet	Serif	18–20	Italic	Left

Figure 1.16 Text style reference sheet

Style

This means the name given to the different elements that make up a style. For example, the heading given in Figure 1.16 has a sans-serif font, the size of which is between 44 and 60 points; it should be displayed in bold and be centred. Each time a piece of text is required in the heading style then it should have all these requirements. This saves writing out the various components each time.

Font

The font refers to the typeface that is being used. There are two types of font – serif and sans-serif. You will need to know the difference between these fonts.

Serif fonts have small strokes (serifs) at the top and/or bottom of some letters that help guide the reader's eye across the page. The text you are reading now is in a serif font. One of the most common serif fonts is **Times New Roman**.

Sans-serif fonts are 'without' serifs – the strokes at the top or bottom of certain letters. These fonts are best used for headings and points of emphasis, as large blocks of sans-serif text can be difficult to read. Sans-serif fonts are ideal for slide presentations which generally contain only a small amount of well displayed text. A common sans-serif font is **Arial**.

Look at Figure 1.17 to see the difference.

This is a serif font – look at the strokes at the bottom of letters, l, m and k.

This is a sans-serif font – there are no strokes at the bottom of letters l, m and k.

Figure 1.17   Serif and sans-serif fonts

There are many different fonts, both serif and sans-serif. It is important to be able to tell the difference between the two. A selection of fonts is shown in Figure 1.18. Study these so that you become familiar with the two types.

This is Baskerville – it is a serif font.
This is Courier – a serif font.
This is Franklin Gothic – a sans-serif font.
This is Futura – a sans-serif font.
This is Garamond – a serif font.
This is Helvetica – a sans-serif font.

Figure 1.18   Different fonts

Change the font

Change the heading font style to a sans-serif font.

Method

1 Click in the placeholder entitled **Click to edit Master Title Style**. You do not have to highlight the text but the cursor should be flashing within the placeholder.

2 Go to the **Font** box 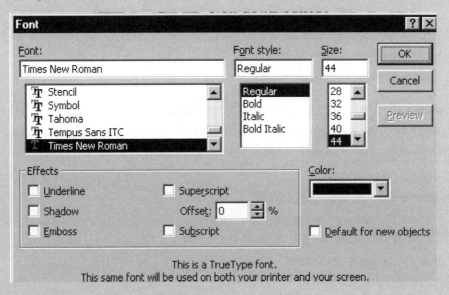 on the toolbar.
3 Click on the arrow at the right-hand side of the box. A drop-down menu of font names will be displayed.
4 Scroll through the fonts until you find one you would like to use. Remember it must be a sans-serif font.
5 Click on the name of the font you want to use. The name will appear in the Font box.

OR

1 Click in the placeholder entitled **Click to edit Master Title Style**.
2 From the **Format** menu, Select: **Font**. The **Font** dialogue box will appear on screen (Figure 1.19).

Figure 1.19 Font sub-menu

3 Key in the name of the font you want to use, *or* scroll down the drop-menu and choose one.
4 Ensure that the name of the font appears in the box. Click on: **OK**.

Size

This refers to the point size of the font you are using. When preparing slide presentations you will need to use larger fonts than you would for word processing a letter or report. As with all design work, it is usual for the heading font size to be the largest, then the sub-heading with the body text using the smallest font size.

Change the size

Exercise 1.14

Change the size of the heading text to a point size of 44.

Method

1 Click in the box entitled **Click to edit Master Title Style**.
2 Click on the arrow to the right-hand side of the **Size** box on the toolbar. A drop-down menu of sizes will appear.
3 Click on point size 44. It will now appear in the size box.

OR

1 Click in the box entitled **Click to edit Master Title Style**.
2 From the **Format** menu, Select: **Font**. The **Font** dialogue box will appear on screen.
3 Key in the size of the font you want to use, *or* scroll down the drop-down menu and choose one.
4 Ensure that the correct size appears in the box. Click on: **OK**.

Emphasis

This means the enhancements that can be made to text such as bold, italic, underscore or a combination of these. Too many enhancements can make text difficult to read so it is better to use just one or possibly two at most.

The main emphasis option buttons are shown in Figure 1.20. These are found on the toolbars. Figure 1.21 shows the effects of the different text emphasis options.

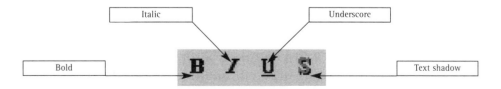

Figure 1.20 Emphasis keys

Bold – This darkens the text to make a display point.

Italic – The text slants to the right. Too much italic text on a presentation makes it rather difficult to read unless the point size is large.

<u>Underscore</u> – This underlines text – use only sparingly as it looks rather old-fashioned and can be difficult to read.

Text Shadow – This gives a 3D appearance and is good for headings, etc.

Figure 1.21 Text emphasis options

Add emphasis

Exercise 1.15

Embolden the heading text.

Method

1 Click in the placeholder entitled **Click to edit Master Title Style**.

2 Click on the Bold icon **B** on the toolbar.

OR

1 Click in the placeholder entitled **Click to edit Master Title Style**.
2 From the **Format** menu, select: **Font**. The **Font** dialogue box will appear on screen.
3 Select the **Bold** option from the **Font Style box**.
4 Ensure that the correct emphasis appears in the box. Click on: **OK**.

Alignment

The alignment of the text means its position on the slide. In order for the alignment to be accurate, the text box you draw will need to stretch from edge to edge across the page. However, you will need to leave a small amount of space on each side as a margin as you will be printing these slides later.

The alignment options are shown in Figure 1.22. These are found on the toolbars. Figure 1.23 shows the effects of the different alignment options.

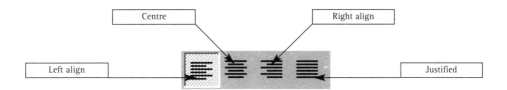

Figure 1.22   Alignment options

Left align
This means the text is aligned at the left-hand margin. The lines are ragged at the right-hand margin as shown in this example. This is the most widely used setting as it is the most easy to read.

Centre
Each line is centred for this option. Used for headings and displays.

Right align
This option aligns text to the right-hand margin. The left-hand margin will be ragged. This option is not used very often, but can be useful for addresses.

Justified
This means that the text is aligned at both the left and the right-hand margins. This is useful for reports, column displays and for making work look neat. However large blocks of justified text can be difficult to read.

Figure 1.23   Text alignment

Change the alignment

Exercise 1.16

Change the alignment of the heading to centred.

Method

1   Click in the placeholder entitled **Click to edit Master Title Style**.
2   Click on the **Centre** alignment button on the toolbar.
3   The text should now be centred.

You have now completed the style for the title. The slide should look like Figure 1.24.

Figure 1.24   Master title style completed

The text style reference sheet states that you will also need to define styles for bullet text and sub-bullet text. You will now need to set master styles for these.

Bullet style text

Bullets are used to make a display of points and are often used in place of numbers to make a list. Traditional bullet points are round dots that are placed in the middle of the line. However there are a variety of bullet points that can be used to enhance your text displays.

When setting up bullet points, it is important to leave at least one clear space between the bullet point and the text. Look at the example shown in Figure 1.25.

- The bullet points sit in the middle of the text line.
- Each new line has a bullet point.
- You can set various bullets to enhance your display.
- You can set the amount of space between the bullet point and the text.

Figure 1.25   Bullets

Set bullet text style

Exercise 1.17

Set the bullet text style on the master slide.

Method

1   Click on the line that says **Click to edit Master text styles**. You will now be amending the text style for the main text of the slide.
2   Change the font, point size, enhancement (if any) and alignment as shown in the text style reference sheet given as Figure 1.16 using the methods given above.
3   To amend the bullet style go to the **Format** menu on the menu bar and choose: **Bullets and Numbering**. The sub-menu shown in Figure 1.26 will appear.

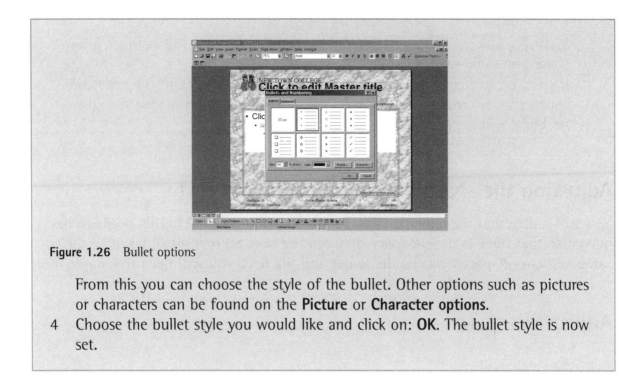

Figure 1.26 Bullet options

From this you can choose the style of the bullet. Other options such as pictures or characters can be found on the **Picture** or **Character options.**

4 Choose the bullet style you would like and click on: **OK.** The bullet style is now set.

Setting a sub-bullet style

You will be required to set a sub-bullet style. Look at the example of a sub-bullet as shown in Figure 1.27.

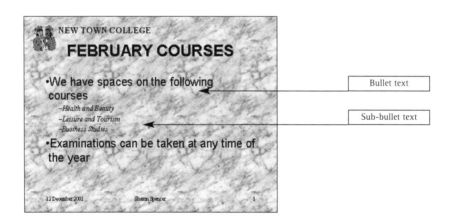

Figure 1.27 Bullet and sub-bullet text

You will see that the sub-bullet text has been indented from the bullet text.

Set sub-bullet text style

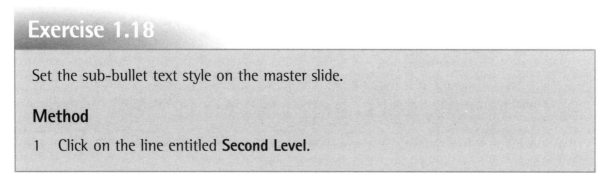

Exercise 1.18

Set the sub-bullet text style on the master slide.

Method

1 Click on the line entitled **Second Level.**

2   Make the various changes to the font and point size using the methods given above and using the reference sheet given as Figure 1.16.

3   If you wish to change the appearance of the bullet – at present the bullet will appear in the form of a dash – make the amendment using the method given for bullet text.

Adjusting the space between bullets and text

You will notice that the bullet is close to the text in Figure 1.27. This needs to be moved so that there is a clear space between the two. So that all slides have the same amount of space between the bullet and the text, you will need to change the space on the master slide.

Adjust the space

Exercise 1.19

Enlarge the space between the bullet point and the text.

Method

1   Ensure that the master slide is on screen. If not, go to **View**, choose: **Master** and then: **Slide Master.**

2   You will need to have the ruler bar on screen so that you can accurately change the spacing. To view the ruler bar, go to **View** and then choose: **Ruler.**

3   To amend the size, you must click on the **Click to edit Master text styles** text.

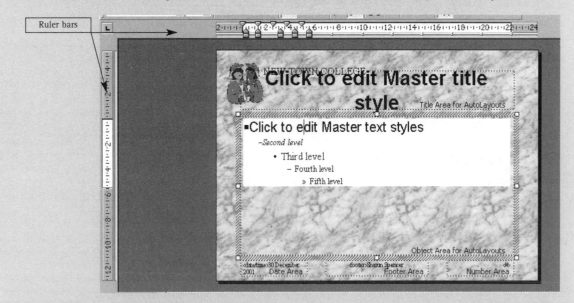

Figure 1.28   Adjusting the space between bullets and text

4   The screen should now look like Figure 1.28.

5   The ruler bar will now display the markers as shown in Figure 1.29.

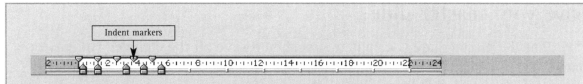

Figure 1.29   Indent markers

6   Move the bottom half of the indent marker to increase the space between the bullet point and the text. A space of around 50–75 mm is sufficient.

7   Deselect the text box by clicking outside the box.

The text styles have now been set in the master slide. You should now close the master slide and return to Slide view.

Close the master slide

Exercise 1.20

Close the master slide using the close box  displayed on the screen.

Method

1   Click on the word **Close**. It is important that you click on the word **Close** rather than use the **X** at the top right-hand corner. This is because if you use the **X** then the **close box** will close the presentation rather than the master slide.

2   You will be taken back to Slide view, which should look like Figure 1.30.

Figure 1.30   Slide view

Note: If the master slide **close box** is not available on screen, do the following:

To retrieve the master slide **close box**:

1   Go to **View** and choose: **Toolbars**.

2   Select **Master**. The master slide close box will appear on screen.

To close the master slide without using the **close box**:

1   Go to **View**.

2   Choose: **Normal**. The view will return to normal.

Save your master slide

Now that the master slide is complete you should save all the changes you have made.

Exercise 1.21

Save the master slide using the filename **COLLEGE1**.

Method

1 Go to the **File** menu on the toolbar.
2 Choose: **Save As**. The **Save As** box will appear on screen.
3 Key in **COLLEGE1** in the **File name** box.
4 Check that you are saving the file in the correct directory. To check this look at the **Save in** box at the top of the screen. If you are not in the correct directory, use the arrow at the right-hand side to move around your folders and directories until you find the correct one. This also applies if you are saving to a floppy disk or CD-ROM.
5 Click on: **Save**.
6 Close the presentation by going to **File** and then **Close**.

Skills Practice 1

Using the following reference sheet, set up a presentation as instructed.

Instructions for master slide style		
Component	**Input**	**Additional information**
Background	One used consistently throughout presentation	Ensure legibility of text against background on printout
Company name	LABRADOR RESCUE	Font: Default
Date	Today's date	Font: Default
Your name	Insert your name	Font: Default
Slide numbering	Insert slide numbers	Font: Default
Company logo	Suitable graphic from Clip Art	

Instructions for text styles

Style	Font	Size	Emphasis	Alignment
Heading	Sans-serif	36–60	Bold	Centre
Bullet	Serif	30–40	Default	Left
Sub-bullet	Serif	22–32	Italic	Left

Design a master slide from the instructions given. Save as **LAB1** and close the presentation.

Skills Practice 2

Using the following reference sheet, set up a presentation as instructed.

Instructions for master slide style

Component	Input	Additional information
Background	One used consistently throughout presentation	Ensure legibility of text against background on printout
Company name	AB TRAINING	Font: Default
Date	Today's date	Font: Default
Your name	Insert your name	Font: Default
Slide numbering	Insert slide numbers	Font: Default
Company logo	Suitable graphic from Clip Art	

Instructions for text styles

Style	Font	Size	Emphasis	Alignment
Heading	Serif	40–60	Bold	Centre
Bullet	Serif	32–38	Italic	Left
Sub-bullet	Sans-serif	22–30	Italic	Left

Design a master slide from the instructions given. Save as **SERVICE1** and close the presentation.

Creating four slides using the master slide

In this section you will learn how to:

- key in text
- add a new slide
- produce an organisation chart.

You are now ready to create the slides that will form the presentation.

Key in text

Exercise 1.22

Key in the following on to Slide 1:

Heading	JANUARY COURSES
Bullet	A Levels – Business Studies, Art and Maths
Bullet	GCSEs – Geography, Maths and Graphics
Bullet	Languages – Beginner's French and Italian
Bullet	Leisure – Navigation, Wine Tasting and Stained Glass

Method

1 Load PowerPoint and open the presentation **COLLEGE1**.
2 Click in the **Click to add Title** placeholder so that the cursor appears.
3 Key in the required text – make sure you use the capitalisation shown on the examination paper. Note that as you type the text also appears in the outline pane on the left-hand side of the screen.
4 Now click in the **Click to add text** placeholder. Key in the text as shown above. The slide should look like Figure 1.31.

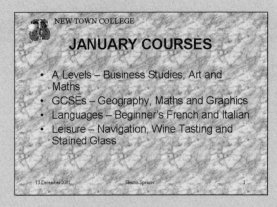

Figure 1.31   Completed slide

Add a new slide

You now need to add a new slide to the presentation.

Exercise 1.23

Insert Slide 2 into the presentation.

Method

1 Go to **Insert** on the menu bar.
2 Click on: **New Slide**. The **New Slide** sub-menu will appear. Click on the **bulleted list** icon. A new slide will appear on screen and the number 2 will appear on the left-hand side.

OR

Click on the **New Slide** icon on the toolbar. The **New Slide** menu will appear on screen. Follow the instructions given above.

Exercise 1.24

Using the methods shown above add the following text to Slide 2. *Note*: Ensure that the cursor is on the last slide in the presentation before inserting a new slide. If you do not then a slide will be inserted wherever the cursor is placed.

Slide number	Style	Text/graphic
2	Heading	MISSION STATEMENT
	Bullet	We aim to provide a high standard of education
	Bullet	Access to new technology will be available to all students
	Bullet	Our examination results will always be above the national average

Exercise 1.25

Add Slide 3 to the presentation. Key in the following text.

Slide number	Style	Text/graphic
3	Heading	THE STUDENT UNION
	Bullet	All students are members of the Student Union
	Bullet	The Student Union organises a number of activities and events throughout the year
	Bullet	The Student Union works with the Senior Management Team to ensure the college meets the needs of students

Organisation charts

You may be asked to produce an organisation chart for your presentation. These are generally used to show the various managers or departments contained within a company. However they can also be used as a framework for flow charts, etc.

PowerPoint has a facility to create organisation charts automatically. This is very useful as it ensures that the boxes and lines created are consistent and accurate. It also saves a great deal of time.

Produce an organisation chart

Exercise 1.26

Add Slide 4 to the presentation and produce an organisation chart as shown in Figure 1.32.

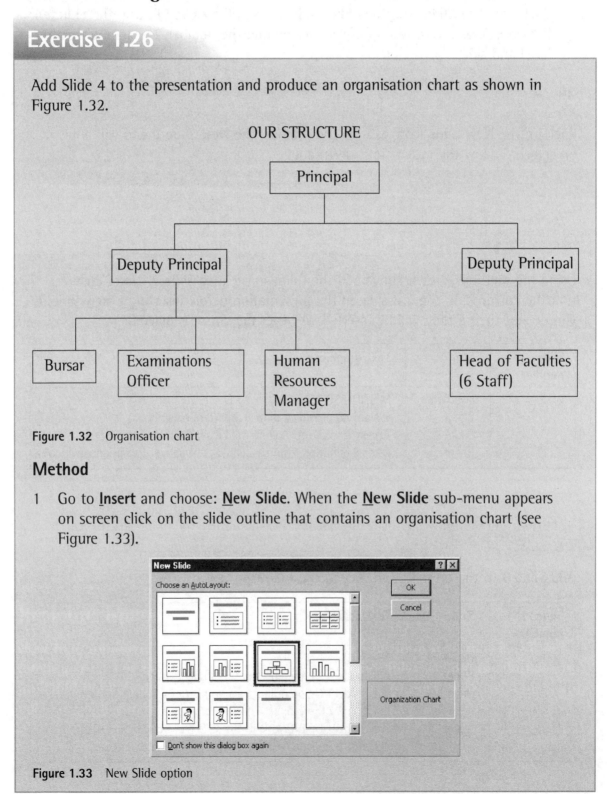

Figure 1.32 Organisation chart

Method

1 Go to **Insert** and choose: **New Slide**. When the **New Slide** sub-menu appears on screen click on the slide outline that contains an organisation chart (see Figure 1.33).

Figure 1.33 New Slide option

Note: The words 'Organization Chart' appear at the right-hand side of the menu.

2   Click on: **OK.**
3   The slide as shown in Figure 1.34 will appear.

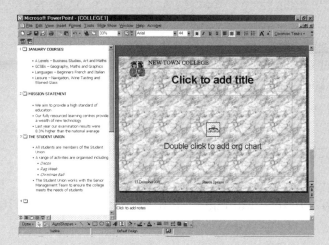

Figure 1.34   Organisation chart placeholder

4   Enter the heading **OUR STRUCTURE** into the title placeholder.
5   Double-click on the icon as instructed on screen. You will be taken to a template of an organisation chart (see Figure 1.35).

Note: If you leave the organisation chart and return to the slide, the icon will have disappeared. In order to return to the organisation chart, double-click in the main text box.

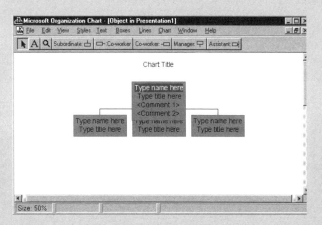

Figure 1.35   Organisation chart

6   In order to enter text into the organisation chart, you must highlight one of the lines of text called 'Type heading here' or 'Type Title here'. It is better to delete the existing text in either of these lines before keying in so that you have a clear line to work with.

When you wish to key text in the lines marked <comment 1> or <comment 2>, you will need to click on these lines and then start to type – you cannot delete these lines manually.

Key in the word **Principal** in the heading space in the top box of the chart. Highlight the line 'Type Title Here' and press: **Delete**. The line should now change to the following: **<Title>**. If you do not do this the line 'Type Title Here' will be imported on to your slide. Now key in the words **Deputy Principal** in the left-hand and middle boxes. Again, you will need to delete the lines 'Type Title Here'.

7   Click in the right-hand text box. You do not need this for the organisation chart and so it must be deleted. To do this, go to **Edit** in the chart window and choose: **Cut**. The text box will disappear.

Adding boxes to the organisation chart

You will need to add some extra boxes to the organisation chart. These are known as Subordinates, Co-workers, Managers and Assistants. Figure 1.36 shows the various options.

Figure 1.36   Organisation chart boxes

You can see that the box you need to use depends on where you will be placing the box. For example, if you were to add a manager, then the box will be placed above an existing box, a subordinate below.

Deleting boxes

If you decide to delete a box at any point, do the following.

Exercise 1.27

Method

1   Click on the box to select it.
2   Go to **Edit** and choose: **Cut**. The box should disappear.

Add subordinate boxes

Exercise 1.28

Add subordinate boxes to the organisation chart.

Method

1   Ensure the organisation chart is loaded correctly.
2   Click on the correct icon – you will need the **subordinate icon** for this exercise.

3   Click on the left-hand box called 'Deputy Principal'. The cursor will change to show a subordinate box. Click to place the subordinate box.

4   Repeat until the left-hand deputy principal has three subordinates and the right-hand deputy principal has one.

5   Add the various names to the boxes as shown in Figure 1.32. In order to display the names as above you will have to key in each line separately. For example:

Key in **Examinations** in the <Name> space.
Key in **Officer** in the <Title> space.

If you do not do this then the names will spread out and you may run out of room.

Note: If you accidentally place a new box incorrectly, then just click on the box, and go to **Edit** and **Cut**. The box will be removed.

The organisation chart is now complete. However if your software displays the organisation chart boxes in green (or any other colour) you will have to modify this. Although the coloured boxes make a good display feature on screen, they will use a lot of ink when printing. If you do not have a colour printer then the printer will substitute a grey tone for the coloured area. There is a possibility of the grey tone being so dark that the text is not legible. It is therefore safer to remove the fill colour altogether.

The border of the box should be printed in black and be of a solid line (not dotted or dashed).

You will also need to remove the text 'chart title' from the organisation chart so that this does not print.

Remove chart title and change the fill colour

Change the fill colour of the organisation chart boxes to 'no fill', change the colour of the border of the boxes to a solid black line and delete the heading 'chart title'.

Method

1   To remove the chart title, simply highlight the text and press: **Delete**.

2   To change the box fill colour, click in the middle of a box, go to **Boxes** on the menu bar and choose: **Color**. A colour chart will appear. Choose the **No Fill** option icon, which looks like Figure 1.37.

Figure 1.37   Color palette

3   Click on: **OK.**

Note: A quick way to change all the boxes at once is as follows. Go to **Edit** on the chart menu. Go to **Select** and choose: **All.**

4   To change the colour of the box border, go to **Boxes** on the menu bar and choose **Border Color**. A colour palette as shown in Figure 1.37 will appear. Choose: black. Click on: **OK.**

5   To ensure that the border is a solid line, go to **Boxes** and choose **Border Line Style**. Ensure that the solid line diagram has a tick by it. If it does not, click on the correct line style.

6   Now click on the close box icon **X** in the top right-hand corner of the screen. The menu as shown in Figure 1.38 will appear.

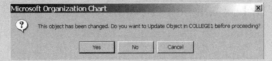

Figure 1.38   Organisation chart close box

Choose: **Yes.** The organisation chart should now appear on the slide.

Printing individual slides and an outline view

In this section you will learn how to save and print the presentation.

You have now finished Document 1 of the examination. You are asked to print one slide per page and an outline view. The outline view will print the outline pane as shown on the computer screen.

Save the presentation

Exercise 1.30

Save the presentation and print one slide per page.

Method

1   Go to **File** and choose: **Print**. The menu as shown in Figure 1.39 will appear.
2   Ensure that, in the **Print range** section, the **All** button is on so that all the slides in the presentation are printed. You should also check that the word 'Slides' appears in the **Print what** box.
3   In order to ensure the background pattern or colour are printed on your slide, you must ensure that the **Grayscale** and **Pure black and white** boxes are *NOT* checked.
4   Once you are sure the settings are correct, click on: **OK.**

Check your work with the example at the back of the book.

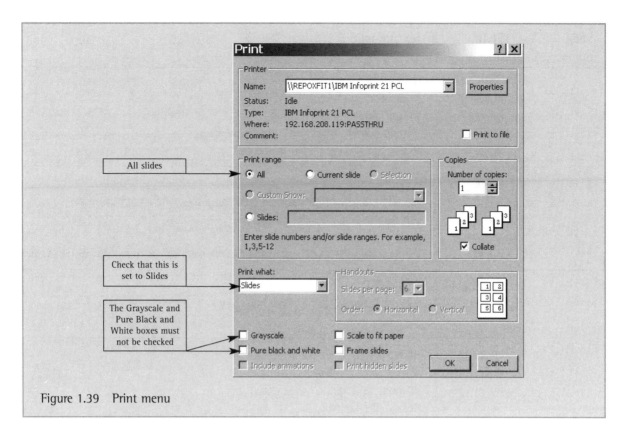

Figure 1.39   Print menu

Print the presentation

Exercise 1.31

Print the slide presentation in an outline view.

Method

1   Go to **File** and choose: **Print**. The menu shown in Figure 1.39 will appear.
2   Ensure that, in the **Print range** section, the **All** button is on so that all the slides in the presentation are printed. In the **Print what** box, change the setting so that it says **Outline View**.
3   Once you are sure the settings are correct, click on: **OK**.
4   Save the presentation as **COLLEGE2** following the instructions given on page 22.

Check your work with the example at the back of the book.

Skills Practice 3

Using the master slide saved as **LAB1**, produce four slides from the information given below retaining capitalisation as shown throughout. Save the presentation as **LAB2**. Print one slide per page and an outline view. Check your work with the example at the back of the book.

Slide number	Style	Text/graphic
1	Heading Bullet Bullet Bullet Bullet	OUR AIMS To provide a home for unwanted or abandoned Labradors To find families for our dogs To help owners train and care for their dogs To assist other centres with the care and re-homing of Labradors
2	Heading Bullet Bullet Bullet	FUNDING We rely entirely on donations from the public and local businesses Our fundraising includes the running of a charity shop in the centre of Bath We need to raise in excess of £50,000 per annum to keep the centre open
3	Heading Insert	THE PEOPLE Insert the organisation chart here. See below for content of chart to be created
4	Heading Bullet Bullet Bullet Bullet Bullet	HOW TO HELP Take a dog for a walk Re-home a dog Help at the kennels Make a donation Help at the shop

Organisation chart for Slide 3

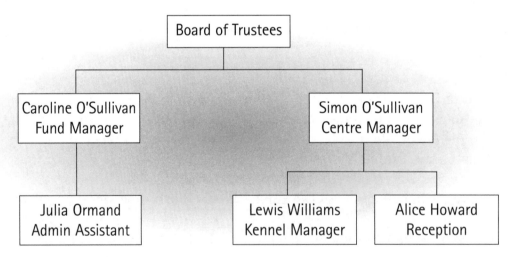

Skills Practice 4

Recall the master slide saved as **SERVICE1**. Using the master slide, produce five slides from the information given below retaining capitalisation as shown throughout. Save the presentation as **SERVICE2**. Print one slide per page and an outline view. Check your work with the example at the back of the book.

Slide number	Style	Text/graphic
1	Heading Bullet Bullet Bullet Bullet	Introduction Customer Service – An Overview Customer Service Policies Internal and External Customers Strategies for dealing with unhappy customers
2	Heading Bullet Bullet Bullet	Overview Customer Service is the key to business success Every member of the company is involved Successful customer service includes internal customers as well as external
3	Heading Bullet Bullet Bullet Bullet	Customer Service Policies A carefully considered customer service policy will ensure success The policy should have clear aims and objectives Policies should be drawn up after consultation with all staff Policies should be easy to implement
4	Heading Bullet Bullet Bullet	Internal and External Customers Internal customers – colleagues External customers – customers of the business Both are equally as important when formulating a customer service policy
5	Heading Insert	Customer Complaint Structure Insert the chart here. See below for content of chart to be created

Chart for Slide 5

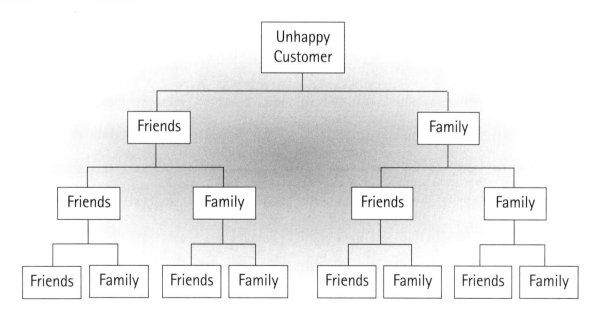

Part 2

This part covers **Document 2** of the examination. This comprises the following:

- Amending slides.
- Printing selected slides.
- Printing audience handouts.

The slides prepared in Document 1 are recalled and amended.

Amending slides

In this section you will learn how to:

- change the bullet style
- amend the text
- add sub-bullets
- alter the size of the placeholder
- add a subordinate.

You may find that you would like to make amendments to your slide presentation. The examination paper will contain a list of amendments that must be made to the various slides. An example of some amendments to **COLLEGE2** is shown in Figure 2.1.

Slide number	Current text	Amendment
Master slide		Change bullet style
2	Access to new technology will be available to all students	Replace with: Our fully resourced learning centres provide a wealth of new technology
2	Our examination results will always be above the national average	Replace with: Last year our examination results were 8.3% higher than the national average
3	The Student Union organises a number of activities and events throughout the year	Replace with: A range of activities are organised including: Add sub-bullet: Discos Add sub-bullet: Rag Week Add sub-bullet: Christmas Ball
4	Add a further subordinate to the Deputy Principal on the right-hand side of the chart	Add: New Business Manager

Figure 2.1   Example amendment sheet

As you will see the amendments to each slide have been clearly set out. The first set of amendments, to the master slide, requires you to change the style of the bullet. This means that the bullet style will be changed on all the slides in your presentation.

Change the bullet style

Exercise 2.1

Change the bullet style on the master slide called **COLLEGE2**.

Method

1 Load the presentation called **COLLEGE2**.
2 Go to **View** and choose: **Slide Master**.
3 Your master slide will appear on screen. Place the cursor in the main text box and right click and choose: **Bullets and Numbering** or go to **Format** and choose: **Bullets and Numbering**. The screen as shown in Figure 2.2 will appear.

Figure 2.2   Bullets and Numbering menu

4 Choose a bullet style you would like by clicking on the picture. If you would like to use a different bullet from those shown, click on: **Picture** or **Character**. You can also change the colour of the bullet by using the colour drop-down menu.
5 Once you have decided which bullet to use, click on: **OK**. The bullet style will change on the master slide and should automatically change all the bullets contained on the slides. However you should check this manually as errors will be penalised.

The second amendment asks you to amend the text contained on Slide 2.

Amend the text

Exercise 2.2

Amend Slide 2 changing the text as shown.

Method

1 Load the presentation and call up Slide 2. To do this, click on the Slide 2 icon on the left-hand side of the page.

2 Highlight the line of text you wish to amend.
3 Key in the new text. It will change on the slide and the outline view will automatically be updated. The slide should now look like Figure 2.3.

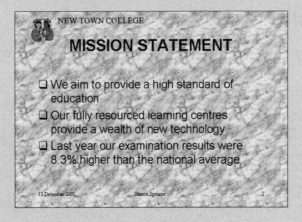

Figure 2.3 Amended slide

Add sub-bullets

Exercise 2.3

Amend Slide 3 adding sub-bullets as shown.

Method

1 Click on the Slide 3 icon to view it. Amend the existing text using the method shown above.
2 Starting a new line for each sub-bullet, key in the text given in the amendment sheet.
3 Highlight all the sub-bullet text and press the **Demote** button ➡ which can be found on the toolbar. The text will move into place and take on the style of the sub-bullet which was set on the master slide.
4 Your slide should now look like Figure 2.4.

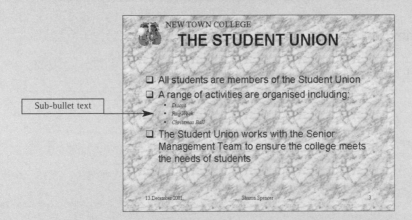

Figure 2.4 Sub-bullet text

Note: To move sub-bullets back to bullet text, use the **Promote** key ⬅.

Altering the size of placeholders

If you key in more text than the size of the placeholder can accept then the following may happen:

1 The text will not be displayed (or printed) in full.
2 The size of the text will be changed to enable the text to fit the placeholder.

Either of these options would incur penalties in the examination and so you must check your work carefully to ensure that all text is displayed.

If the text has not been displayed or has changed size you may alter the size of the placeholder in order to accommodate all the text.

Alter the size of the placeholder

Exercise 2.4

Alter the size of the text placeholder on Slide 3.

Method

1 Click on the placeholder so that the handles are shown.
2 Resize the placeholder by clicking on the outline of the placeholder and dragging the box out to the required size. Ensure the box does not fall off the slide at any point.
3 The text should now be reinstated along with the correct text styles. However, you will need to check this very carefully to ensure that all the text styles are present.

Amending the organisation chart

The organisation chart needs a subordinate added.

Add a subordinate

Exercise 2.5

Add a subordinate to the existing organisation chart on Slide 4.

Method

1 Click on the Slide 4 icon to view it.
2 Double-click on the organisation chart to get to the organisation chart sub-menu.
3 Click on the subordinate box. The cursor should change to a subordinate box.
4 Click in the Deputy Principal box on the right-hand side of the organisation chart. A new subordinate should appear on screen.

5   Key in the text as shown on the amendment sheet (see Figure 2.5).
6   Close the organisation chart using the **X**. You will be asked if you wish to update the chart on the slide. Click on: **OK**.

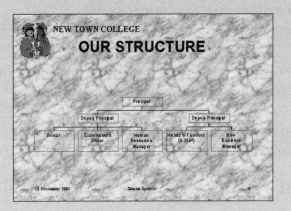

Figure 2.5   Amended organisation chart

Printing selected slides

In this section you will learn how to print the slides.

You will need to print the slides that have been amended.

Print the slides

Exercise 2.6

Print the slides that have been amended (2, 3 and 4).

Method

1   Go to **File**.
2   Go to **Print**.
3   Click in the **Slides** button on the **Print range** box. Key in the slides' numbers separating the numbers with commas.
4   Check that the **Print what** box states **Slides**.
5   Click on: **OK** (see Figure 2.6).

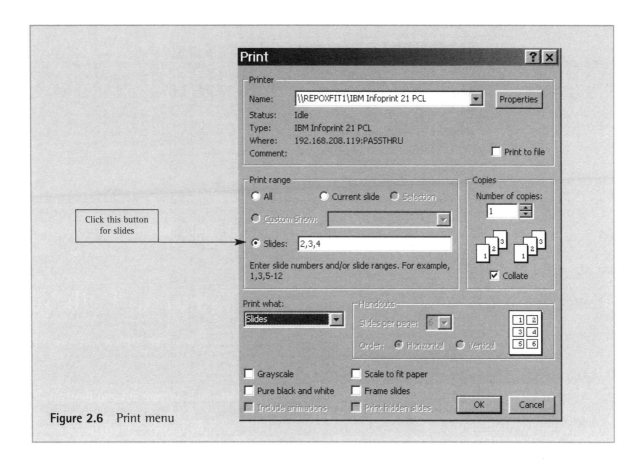

Figure 2.6   Print menu

Printing audience handouts

In this section you will learn how to print audience handouts.

Audience handouts contain a small image of the slides. If you print three slides per page a space to write notes will also appear.

Print audience handouts

Exercise 2.7

Print audience handouts of your presentation.

Method

1   Go to **File**.
2   Go to **Print**.
3   In the **Print range** box click on: **All**.
4   In the **Print what** option choose: **Handouts**.
5   In the **Handouts** box amend the **Slides per page** box to show 3 per page. A sketch of the proposed page will appear. Check that it is correct.
6   Click on: **OK** (see Figure 2.7).

Note: Remember to check that the greyscale option has been turned off.
Check your work with the example at the back of the book.

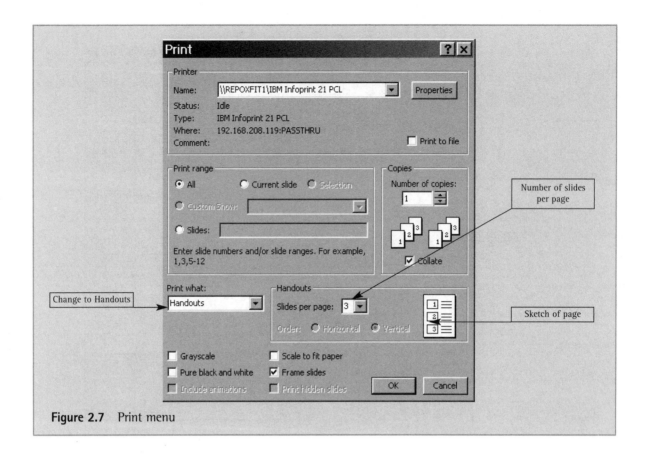

Figure 2.7   Print menu

Exercise 2.8

Save the presentation as **COLLEGE3**.

Skills Practice 5

Recall the presentation saved as **LAB2**. Change the bullet symbol style on the master slide and amend the slides as shown below. Save as **LAB3**. Print all slides as audience handouts (three slides per page). Check your work with the example at the back of the book.

Slide number	Current text	Amendment
Master		Change bullet symbol style
1	To provide a home for unwanted or abandoned Labradors	Replace with: To provide short- or long-term care for unwanted or abandoned Labradors
3	Add a further subordinate to Caroline O'Sullivan	Add: Justin Hope Membership Secretary
3	In the Kennel Manager box	Replace Lewis Williams with Anthony Malik
4	Help at the shop	Add sub-bullet: By donating unwanted items Add sub-bullet: By serving in the shop Add sub-bullet: By collecting items from others

Skills Practice 6

Recall the presentation saved as **SERVICE2**. Change the bullet symbol style on the master slide and amend the slides as shown below. Save as **SERVICE3**. Print all slides as audience handouts (four slides per page). Also print the amended Slide 4 on one full page. Check your work with the example at the back of the book.

Slide number	Current text	Amendment
Master slide		Change bullet symbol style
1	After bullet point Internal and External Customers	Add bullet: Customer Complaint Structure Add bullet: Financial Benefits
2	Every member of the company is involved	Replace with: Successful customer service requires all staff to become involved
4	External customers – customers of the business	Add sub-bullet: Buyers of goods and services Add sub-bullet: Suppliers of goods and services

Part 3

This section covers **Document 3** of the examination. This comprises the following:

- Creating a graph.
- Adding Clip Art to your presentation.
- Printing the graphs.

The slides prepared in Document 2 are recalled and amended.

Creating a graph

In this section you will learn how to:

- create a new slide containing a pie chart
- create a new slide containing a bar chart
- insert a new slide and create a line graph
- save the presentation.

You will need to create a graph for your presentation. PowerPoint has a facility that will automatically create a graph that can be imported into your presentation. Look at the graph shown in Figure 3.1.

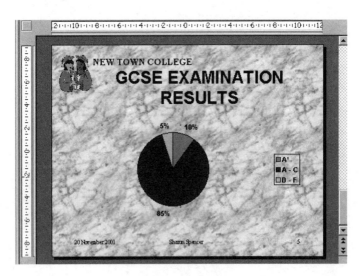

Figure 3.1   Pie chart

This is a pie chart that has been created in PowerPoint and then imported on to a new slide.

Create a new slide containing a pie chart

Exercise 3.1

Create a new slide containing a pie chart from the data given below.

Heading: **GCSE EXAMINATION RESULTS**

Data for pie chart

	A*	A–C	D–F
GCSEs	30	140	8

Method

1 Open the presentation **COLLEGE3** and click on the icon to go to the last slide in the presentation.
2 Go to **Insert** and choose: **New Slide**.
3 From the **New Slide** sub-menu, choose the **Chart** slide which has a large graph area and a heading box. Click on: **OK** (see Figure 3.2).

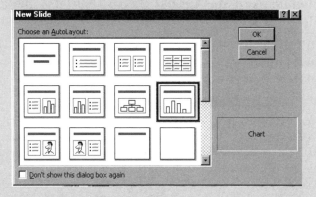

Figure 3.2 Chart slide option

4 The template shown in Figure 3.3 will appear. Insert the heading given above in the Title placeholder.

Figure 3.3 Chart template

5 **Double-click** on the chart icon. You will be taken to the table shown in Figure 3.4.

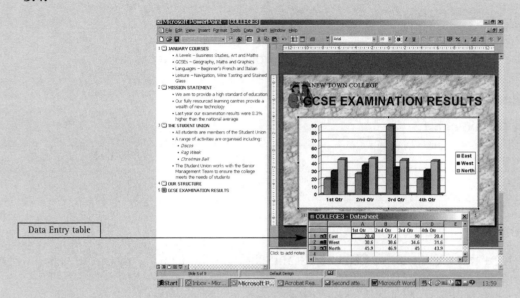

Figure 3.4 Data Entry table

You will see that a Data Entry table appears and a sample graph is placed on the slide. The default setting is for bar chart so the first thing you need to do is change to a pie chart format.

6 Go to **Chart** on the menu bar and choose: **Chart Type**. A chart dialogue box will appear (see Figure 3.5).

Figure 3.5 Chart Type sub-dialogue box

7 Choose: **Pie**. The sub-menu shown in Figure 3.6 will appear.
8 Choose the type of pie chart you would like by clicking on one of the diagrams contained in the **Chart sub-type** to the right of the menu. When you have chosen, click on: **OK**.

Figure 3.6 Pie Chart sub-menu

9 Now you need to enter the data in order to create the pie chart. The first thing you should do is delete the existing data and text so that you have a clear box to work with. To delete the text, click on the boxes at the top of the data table (see Figure 3.7) and drag the cursor down and across to highlight all the text. Once this is highlighted press: **Delete**. All the text should now be removed.

| Click on the top row of boxes |

JANUARY COURSES - Datasheet		A	B	C	D	E
		1st Qtr	2nd Qtr	3rd Qtr	4th Qtr	
1	East	20.4	27.4	90	20.4	
2	West	30.6	38.6	34.6	31.6	
3	North	45.9	46.9	45	43.9	
4						
5						

Figure 3.7 Data Entry table

10 To enter the data click in the boxes and enter the data as shown (see Figure 3.8). To move from box to box press the tab key.

COLLEGE3 - Datasheet		A	B	C	D	E
		A*	A - C	D - F		
1	GCSEs					
2						
3						
4						

Figure 3.8 Data Entry table

11 Once you have finished entering the data, click on the **Slide**. The graph will now be complete and should look like Figure 3.9.

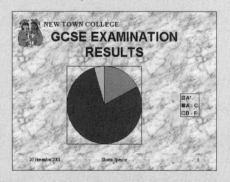

Figure 3.9 Completed graph

Note: If you lose the Chart Data Entry table from the screen whilst you are working on the graph then click on the **View Datasheet** icon 🔲 . The Data Entry table will reappear. If you have finished working on the graph and need to view the Data Entry table, then double-click on the chart – the Data Entry table will reappear.

Amending the graph

Although the graph is complete you need to ensure that labels showing the percentage figures are added to the graph. These should appear next to the relevant sector of the pie. Labels showing the legend may also be required and these may either be displayed as a legend or next to the relevant sector, depending on the instruction given in the examination paper. You may also wish to take off the border around the pie chart to give a neater appearance.

Add percentage labels

Exercise 3.2

Amend the labels to show the percent value in the label next to the relevant pie sector and to ensure that the legend is not displayed separately.

Method

1   Double-click on the pie chart to bring up the data table and graph menu options.
2   Click on: **Chart** from the toolbar and choose: **Chart Options**. The menu shown in Figure 3.10 will appear.

Figure 3.10   Chart Option menu

3   Click on the tab labelled **Data Labels**. The menu shown in Figure 3.11 will appear.

Figure 3.11   Data Label sub-menu

4   Choose the **Show label and percent** button to ensure that both the label and the value are displayed next to the relevant pie sector.
5   Click on the tab labelled **Legend** and click off the **Show Legend** box at the top of the dialogue box. Click on: **OK**.

Remove the border lines

Exercise 3.3

If border lines appear around the pie chart, as shown in Figures 3.10, 3.11 and 3.12 (the lines that sit tightly to the pie chart, forming a square shape), it is best to remove them. The following method shows how to remove the border lines.

Method

1 Double-click on the pie chart to bring up the Data Entry table. The pie chart may have a grey border surrounding it (see Figure 3.12).

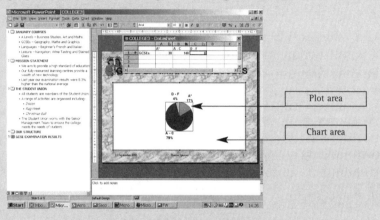

Figure 3.12 Plot area

2 Double-click on the **Plot Area**. The **Format Plot Area** menu will appear (see Figure 3.13).

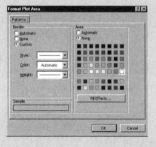

Figure 3.13 Pattern Border sub-menu

3 Click on the **None** button in the **Border** menu.
4 Click on: **OK**.
5 You will be taken back to the Data Entry table and the pie chart will be selected. Click once on the graph to remove the selection.

Create a bar chart

You may have to create a bar chart rather than a pie chart for the examination.

Create a new slide containing a bar chart

Exercise 3.4

Create a new slide containing a bar chart with the heading **RESULT COMPARISON**.

Method

1 Go to **Insert** and choose: **New Slide**.
2 From the **New Slide** sub-menu, choose the **Chart** slide. Click on: **OK**.
3 Key in the heading: **RESULT COMPARISON**.
4 Double-click on the chart icon.
5 As the default setting is for a bar chart there is no need to go to **Chart Type**. However, if you wish to change the appearance of your bar chart, then you can follow the instructions given for pie chart.
6 Clear the data from the data table as outlined above.
7 Enter the following data:

	2001	2000	1999
New Town College	85	80	78
Local Authority	73	78	72
National Average	69	71	70

8 Click off the Data Entry table on to the chart.
9 Now add the axis labels. To do this, go to **Chart** and choose: **Chart Options**. The menu shown in Figure 3.14 will appear.

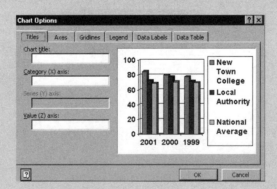

Figure 3.14 Chart Options menu

10 Ensure that the tag **Titles** is selected. Enter the label **Year** in the **Category (X) axis** space.
11 Enter the label **A*–C Grades %** in the **Value (Z) axis**.
12 Click on: **OK**.

The legend should automatically be updated. If you wish to make any changes to your graph then follow the instructions given for the pie chart. Your bar chart should look like Figure 3.15.

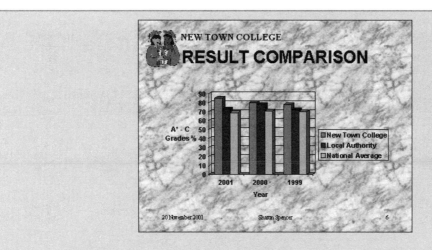

Figure 3.15 Completed bar graph

Check your work with the example at the back of the book.

Create a line graph

You may also have to create a line graph for the examination.

Insert a new slide and create a line graph

Insert a new slide and create a line graph from the data provided. Use the heading: **STUDENT ADMISSIONS**.

Method

1 Go to **Insert** and choose: **New Slide**.
2 From the **New Slide** sub-menu, choose the **Chart** slide. Click on: **OK**.
3 Add the heading: **STUDENT ADMISSIONS**.
4 Double-click on the chart icon.
5 Go to **Chart** on the toolbar and choose: **Chart Type**. Select a **Line graph** and click on: **OK**.
6 Clear the data from the data table as outlined above.
7 Enter the following data:

	2001	2000	1999
GCSEs	200	180	182
A Levels	240	232	175
GNVQ	97	65	31

8 Click off the Data Entry table on to the chart.
9 Now add the axis labels. To do this, go to **Chart** and choose: **Chart Options**.
10 Ensure that the tag **Titles** is selected.
11 Key in: **Year** in the **Category (X) axis**.
12 Key in: **Number of Students** in the **Value (Z) axis**.

12 Click on: **OK.** Your graph will automatically be updated and should look like Figure 3.16.

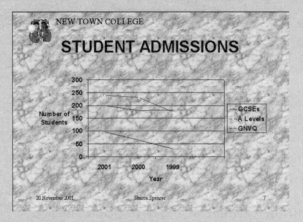

Figure 3.16 Completed line graph

Check your work with the example at the back of the book.

Save the presentation

Save the presentation as **COLLEGE4.**

Adding Clip Art to your presentation

In this section you will learn how to add Clip Art to your presentation.

You added a piece of Clip Art to your master slide. The procedures for adding Clip Art to a slide are the same, although if you use the correct slide template you will automatically be taken to the Clip Art menu.

Add Clip Art to your presentation

Exercise 3.7

Insert a new slide containing text and an image.

Slide number	Style	Text
8	Picture	Import an appropriate Clip Art
	Heading	ENROLMENT
	Bullet	You can enrol by phone, fax, email or in person
	Bullet	Enrolment times are between 8.30 am and 8.00 pm
	Bullet	Reduced rates available. Ask for details

Method

1 Insert a new slide, choosing one of the two **Clip Art & Text** templates (see Figure 3.17).

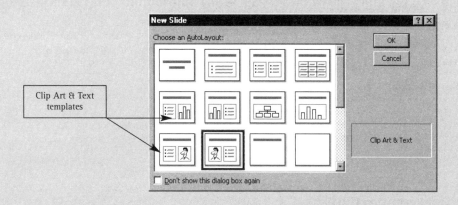

Figure 3.17 Clip Art template

2 Key in the heading and bullet text in the appropriate placeholders.
3 Click on the **Clip Art Icon**. You will automatically be taken to the Clip Art menu.
4 Choose an appropriate image and import into the slide.
5 You may need to resize the image. To do this, look at page 11.
6 Your slide should look similar to Figure 3.18.

Figure 3.18 Completed slide

Printing multiple slides on one sheet

In this section you will learn how to:

- print on one sheet of paper
- save your presentation.

Print on one sheet of paper

Exercise 3.8

Print Slides 7 and 8 on one sheet.

Method

1 Go to **Print** on the **File** menu.
2 Ensure **Slides** is checked in the **Print range** box.
3 Key in: 7–8 as the slide range.
4 Ensure that **Handouts** is showing in the **Print what** box.
5 In the Handouts box, change **Slides per page** to **2**.
6 Click on: **OK**.

Check your work with the example at the back of the book.

Save your presentation

Exercise 3.9

Save your presentation as **COLLEGE5**.

Skills Practice 7

Recall the presentation saved as **LAB3**. Create two further slides from the information given below retaining capitalisation as shown. The pie chart should display the legend and % data labels. Save as **LAB4**. Print only Slides 5 and 6 on one page. Check your work with the example at the back of the book.

Slide number	Style	Text
5	Heading	SPENDING
	Pie chart	Refer below for data
6	Picture	Import a Clip Art of your choice
	Heading	EVENTS
	Bullet	Christmas Sale
	Bullet	Centre Open Day
	Bullet	Training Classes
	Bullet	Dog Show

Data for pie chart

Food	Salaries	Vet	Operating Costs
45	86	34	21

Skills Practice 8

Recall the presentation saved as **SERVICE3**. Create two further slides from the information given below, retaining capitalisation as shown throughout. The pie chart should display the legend and % data labels. Save as **SERVICE4**. Print only Slides 6 and 7 together on one page. Check your work with the example at the back of the book.

Slide number	Style	Text/graphic
6	Heading	FINANCIAL BENEFITS
	Pie chart	Refer below for data
7	Picture	Import a suitable Clip Art picture
	Heading	STRATEGIES
	Bullet	Listen carefully
	Bullet	If possible, grant request
	Bullet	If not, state what can be done
	Bullet	Use a polite, friendly and firm tone

Data for pie chart

Company A	Company B	Company C	Company D
33	45	65	14

Part 4

This section covers **Document 4** of the examination. This comprises the following:

- Deleting slides.
- Adding speaker's notes to slides.
- Changing the order of the slides.
- Printing the speaker's notes.

The slides prepared in Document 3 are recalled and amended.

Deleting slides

In this section you will learn how to delete slides.

If you decide to delete one of your slides in the presentation you can easily remove the slide and its contents by using the following method.

Delete slides

Exercise 4.1

Delete Slides 6 and 7 from the presentation **COLLEGE5**.

Method

1   Using the **Outline pane** on the left-hand slide (see Figure 4.1), click on the icon for Slide 6.

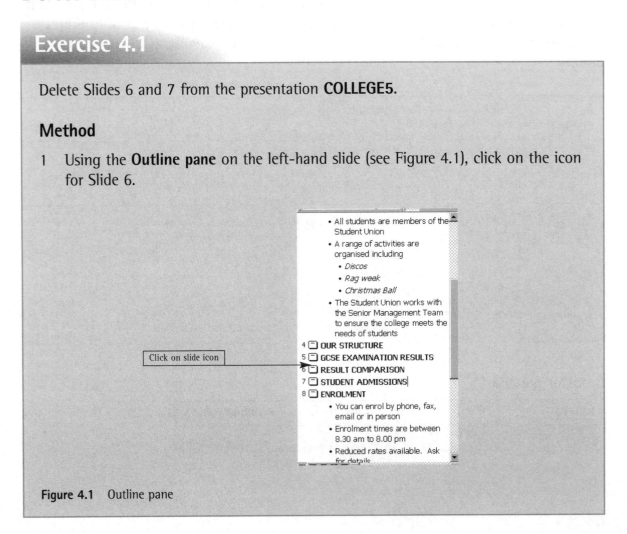

Figure 4.1   Outline pane

2   Go to **Edit** and choose: **Cut**.
3   PowerPoint will ask you if you are sure you wish to delete the slide and its contents.
4   Click on: **Yes**.

Note: When you have deleted a slide, PowerPoint automatically renumbers all the slides left in the presentation. This means that once you have deleted Slide 6, Slide 7 will become Slide 6. Remember to check carefully the contents of the slide before you delete it.

Adding speaker's notes to slides

In this section you will learn how to:

*   add speaker's notes
*   key in notes
*   proofread and spell check.

If you are going to give a presentation, you may need to have extra speaker's notes to expand upon the bullet points. These can be added to the presentation and printed alongside the appropriate slide. They will not be present on the slide presentation.

Add speaker's notes

Exercise 4.2

Add speaker's notes to each slide.

Method

1   Ensure Slide 1 is on screen.
2   Click in the **Click to add notes** pane at the bottom of the screen.
3   To increase the size of the notes pane so that you can see the text whilst you are keying in, click on the bar as shown in Figure 4.2. Drag the bar upwards so that the notes space increases.

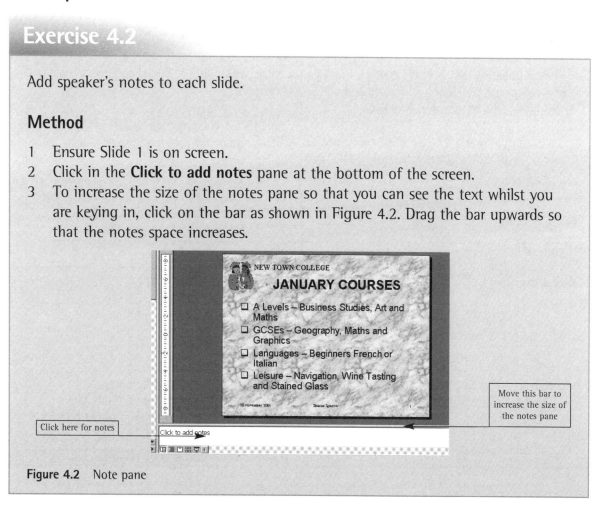

Figure 4.2   Note pane

4   Add the following notes ensuring that the headings are emphasised with bold and capitalisation is followed:

Slide 1
JANUARY COURSES We offer a range of courses starting in January including A Levels and GCSEs. These will run for five terms with the examinations being taken at the end of the fifth term. Our language courses are perfect for those hoping to holiday abroad. If you find you enjoy studying a foreign language we offer intermediate and advanced courses beginning in September. The leisure courses listed here are only a small selection of the wide range on offer. Why not pick up one of our leisure course booklets and choose a new hobby or interest?

Check your work with the example at the back of the book (see example for Exercise 4.6, Slide 1).

Key in notes

Exercise 4.3

Key in the following notes for the slides contained in your presentation.

Slide 2	Slide 3
MISSION STATEMENT We have spent over £50,000 during the past year on updating the three ICT centres. Thirty new computers have been purchased and all computers now have Internet access. Our examination results have been improving year on year and we are now recognised as one of the top performing centres in the local area.	THE STUDENT UNION The Student Union is thriving at New Town College with many activities and events taking place each term. Students are encouraged to take part in the wide-ranging activities organised by the Student Union. Last year the Student Union raised over £10,000 for local and national charities.

Slide 4	Slide 5
OUR STRUCTURE The Senior Management Team meet weekly to discuss college issues. The Team work together to ensure the college continues to provide the best possible education for its students.	GCSE EXAMINATION RESULTS The GCSE results were outstanding with the majority of students gaining a minimum of 5 GCSEs at grades A*–C. We are sure that the excellent results are linked to the progressive teaching methods, well resourced ICT centre and commitment of both staff and students.

Slide 6
ENROLMENT We always have helpful and friendly staff on hand to help you enrol on the most suitable course for your needs. If you would like further advice, please contact the Student Services Officer.

Using the spellcheck facility

Once you have keyed in the text, you should always remember to proofread and spell check your work. Read through the text carefully to ensure you have not missed any words out and then use the spellcheck facility to ensure that all words are spelt correctly.

Proofread and spell check

Exercise 4.4

Proofread the text and use the spellcheck facility.

Method

1 Check the text you have keyed in against the printed examination form to ensure that nothing has been missed.
2 Go to **Tools** and choose: **Spelling**. Alternatively, press: **F7**. The spellcheck will automatically check your document.
3 If you have made an error, check the options you are given (see Figure 4.3). Choose the correct option – be careful here: the correct option is not always the first option. To choose an option, click on the word you wish to use.

Figure 4.3   Spelling options

4 When you are sure you have chosen the correct word, click on: **Change**. The spellcheck will close automatically once it has finished checking the text.

Changing the order of the slides

In this section you will learn how to change the order of the slides.

You may, after looking through your presentation, decide to change the order of the slides. This easy to do with PowerPoint.

Change the order of the slides

Exercise 4.5

Change the order of the slides so that Slide 5 becomes Slide 3.

Method

1   On the outline pane, click on the icon of the slide you wish to move and hold down. The cursor will change to a four-arrow cursor and the slide title will be highlighted.
2   Drag the slide to the correct position, so that it is below Slide 2. The slide will automatically move to the correct position.

OR

1   Go to **View** and change to **Slide Sorter.** The view as shown in Figure 4.4 will appear on screen.
2   Click on the slide you wish to move. In Figure 4.4 slide 5 has a dark box around it which shows it has been highlighted.
3   Drag the slide to the correct position.

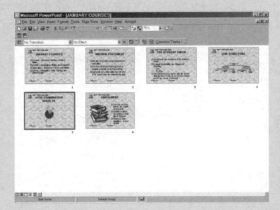

Figure 4.4   Slide Sorter view

Printing the speaker's notes

In this section you will learn how to:

- print speaker's notes
- save the presentation.

You need to print the speaker's notes that have been keyed in showing the slides in the correct order.

Print speaker's notes

Exercise 4.6

Print speaker's notes for the entire presentation.

Method

1 Go to **Print**.
2 In the **Print what** box change to **Notes Pages**.
3 Ensure that **All** is switched on in the **Print range** box.
4 Click on: **OK**.

Check your work with the example at the back of the book.

Save the presentation

Exercise 4.7

Save the presentation as **COLLEGE6**.

Skills Practice 9

Recall the presentation saved as LAB4. Delete the slide containing the organisation chart. Enter the following text as speaker's notes. Ensure the headings on the notes are emphasised with bold and that capitalisation is followed. Please check the spelling of the circled words. Check your work with the example at the back of the book.

Slide 1	Slide 2
OUR AIMS We are one of only three centres in the country that specialise in helping unwanted Labrador dogs. We aim to re-home all the animals that are brought into the centre where possible. However if this is not possible the dogs stay at the rescue center We are keen to promote training classes for owners and their dogs. We help owners understand the needs of their dogs and teach the dogs basic obedence skills.	FUNDING Although we are a registered charity we do not attract any grants from local goverment. We are however, supported by the local community. Our recently opened charity shop in the centre of Bath provides a steady income. The figure of £50,000 increases each year. We need to increase our fundraising activities if our future is to be secure.

Slide 3	Slide 4
HOW TO HELP We are always looking for willing volunters! Dog walkers may take a dog for a walk over the local countryside. If you would like to re-home a dog our staff will help you find the most suitable dog. If you can spare a few hours a week do please help at our shop. If this is not possable then donate items for us to sell. Make a donation. All donations no matter how small make a significant difference to the Labrador Rescue Centre.	SPENDING Our biggest expence each year is salaries for our staff. However the cost of food for the dogs rose by 9% last year. The veterinary expenses are low because our local veterinary surgeon charges only minimal fees as a gesture of goodwill. We are very gratefull for this assistance.

Slide 5
EVENTS The Christmas Sale takes place at the Pavilion on the first Saturday in December each year. The Centre Open Day takes place on the first Sunday in September. Training classes are held on Wedensday evenings throughout the year. The Dog Show, which is held during July attracts visitors from all over the country.

Change the order of the slides so that Slide 4 becomes Slide 3. Save the presentation as **LAB5**. Print the speaker's notes.

Skills Practice 10

Recall the presentation saved as **SERVICE4**. Delete the slide containing the pie chart. Enter the following text as speaker's notes, retaining capitalisation as shown throughout. Ensure the headings on the notes are emphasised with bold. Please check the spelling of the circled words. Check your work with the example at the back of the book.

Slide 1	Slide 2
Introduction Welcome to our Customer Service Training Workshop. I would like to thank you all for coming. The workshop will foccus on finding out what exactly is customer service. We will show you how setting a customer service policy can lead to financial benefits and give you some strategies on how to deal with unhappy customers.	Overview Customer Service is the key to business success. Most companies know that repeat business is the most simple and effective way to make profits. Customer service means so much more than dealing with complaints. A company with an effective customer service policy will rarely have to deal with complaints!

Slide 3	Slide 4
Customer Service Policies Research has shown that every successful business has a carefuly considered customer service policy. The most effective policies are simple and straightforward with clear aims and objectives. Above all, a policy should be easy to implement. It is important to be realistic about the time and training involved in implementing new policies.	Internal and External Customers The customer service ethos is reflected in the way staff communicate and interact. It is important that customer service is management led and that staff are encouraged to play their part in ensuring the workflow is as efficient and effective as possible. Do not forget that the suppliers and contractors who deal with your company on a reguler basis must also be considered to be customers.

Slide 5	Slide 6
Customer Complaint Structure This is what happens when a customer is unhappy with the service they have received from your company. They will tell their family and friends. Their family and friends will tell their family and friends and so on. One very unhappy customer can cost a company hundreds of potential new and satesfied customers. Unfortunately, a happy customer will not normally tell their family and friends in quite the same way. Why? This is because the customer expects to be satisfied with the transaction they have made with your company. ⬇	Strategies One of the easiest and most effective ways of dealing with an unhappy customer is to listen carefully to their complaint. In most situations the customer already knows what they want the outcome of the complaint to be. If their solution is unresonible or unrealistic, say so. However, immediately follow this up with a solution that can be given. Be prepared to negotiate. ⬇

Slide 5 (cont'd)	Slide 6 (cont'd)
The chart shows the drastic effect an unhappy customer can have on a company's reputation.	Use a polite, friendly and firm tone when dealing with unhappy customers. Appear interested and act with confidence and authority.

Change the order of the slides so that Slide 4 becomes Slide 3. Save this document as **SERVICE5**. Print the speaker's notes.

Consolidation 1

Document 1

Using the following reference sheet, set up a presentation as instructed.

Instructions for master slide style		
Component	**Input**	**Additional information**
Background	One used consistently throughout presentation	Ensure legibility of text against background on printout
Company name	CORPORATE GIFTS PLC	Font: Default
Date	Today's date	Font: Default
Your name	Insert your name	Font: Default
Slide numbering	Insert slide numbers	Font: Default
Company logo	Suitable graphic from Clip Art	

Instructions for text styles				
Style	**Font**	**Size**	**Emphasis**	**Alignment**
Heading	Sans-serif	40–60	Bold	Centre
Bullet	Sans-serif	32–38	Default	Left
Sub-bullet	Serif	22–30	Default	Left

Design a master slide from the instructions given. Using the master slide, produce four slides from the information given below retaining capitalisation as shown throughout. Save the presentation as **GIFTS1**. Print one slide per page and an outline view.

Slide number	Style	Text/graphic
1	Heading	ANNUAL FORECAST
	Bullet	This year's profits will decrease by 14% on last year
	Bullet	The profit forecast for the next financial year has been reduced to £2 million
	Bullet	Shareholders' dividends will be reduced by 4% this year
2	Heading	WHAT WENT WRONG?
	Bullet	Rents, overheads and salaries have increased by over 7% during the last year

	Bullet	The launch of our new gift range was postponed because of production difficulties
	Bullet	Nationally consumer confidence has been low
3	Heading	WHAT CAN WE DO?
	Bullet	Hold current expansion plans
	Bullet	Consider further reducing shareholders' dividends
	Bullet	Relocate head office to more economic area
4	Heading	THE FIGURES
	Insert	Insert a bar chart using the data given below
	Label X axis	Year
	Label Z axis	£ million

Data for bar chart

	2000	1999	1998	1997
Income	67	75	72	68.4
Expenditure	64	67	65	61
Profits	3	8	7	7.4

Document 2

Recall the presentation saved as **GIFTS1**. Change the bullet symbol style on the master slide and amend the slides as shown below. Save as **GIFTS2**. Print all slides as audience handouts (three slides per page). Print a copy of the amended Slide 2 on one full page.

Slide number	Current text	Amendment
Master slide		Change bullet symbol style
1	This year's profits will decrease by 14% on last year	Replace with: The profit forecast for this year shows a reduction of 14%
2	Rents, overheads and salaries have increased by over 7% during the last year	Replace with: Expenditure has increased greatly Add sub-bullet: Rents, overheads and salaries by 7% Add sub-bullet: Production costs by 15% Add sub-bullet: Distribution costs by 10%
3	Relocate head office to more economic area	Add: and review management structure
4	See data entry table	Amend figures as shown in table

Change data for bar chart

	2000	1999	1998	1997
Income	67	75	72	68.4
Expenditure	64	60	58	52
Profits	3	15	14	16.4

Document 3

Recall the presentation saved as **GIFTS2**. Create two further slides from the information given below retaining capitalisation as shown. Save as **GIFTS3**. Print only Slides 5 and 6 on one page.

Slide number	Style	Text/graphic
5	Heading Insert	NEW STRUCTURE Insert the organisation chart here. See below for content of chart to be created
6	Picture Heading Bullet Bullet Bullet	Import a Clip Art of your choice NEW RANGE Production difficulties now resolved Due to launch within next eight weeks Projected sales 25% higher than original forecast

Organisation chart for Slide 5

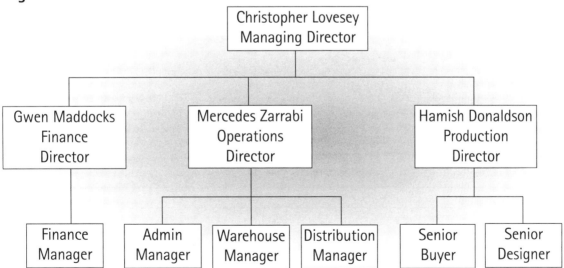

Document 4

Recall the presentation saved as **GIFTS3**. Delete the slide containing the bar chart. Enter the following text as speaker's notes, retaining capitalisation throughout as shown. Ensure the headings on the notes are emphasised with bold. Please check the spelling of the circled words.

Slide 1	Slide 2
ANNUAL FORECAST This year has not matched expectations. The reduction in profits is obviously a matter of some concern. The forecast of a £2 million profit for next year is the lowest projection. It is hoped that if immediate action is taken this can be increased by an additional £1.5 million. Our shareholders will be (dissapointed) with their (dividand) this year, however we are sure that these will increase rapidly over the next few years.	WHAT WENT WRONG? Expenditure has (greatley) increased during the last twelve months. Inflation has risen and all overheads have increased in line. The production problems with our new gift range have now been resolved and the launch will take place shortly. The increase in inflation has affected consumer confidence. We are, however, able to cope with a downturn in business as long as we remain vigilant.

Slide 3	Slide 4
WHAT CAN WE DO? By halting our (expantion) plans we can ensure that we remain financially secure. This will help us through any recession.	NEW STRUCTURE This chart shows the proposed new structure for head office. It is a much leaner structure with a level of management

Slide 3 (cont'd)	Slide 4 (cont'd)
By relocating the head office and reviewing the management structure we are confident that overheads could be reduced by as much as 5% over the next two years.	removed. (Obviously) this will lead to staff (redundancys) but it is hoped that these can be kept to a minimum. The new structure is only in its first draft. Much will depend on the results of the new product launch and whether we decide to relocate head office.

Slide 5

NEW RANGE

The production difficulties we have had with the new range have now been resolved. Although we were disappointed with the setbacks we were given the (oppportunity) to undertake more market research and extra publicity. We have been delighted with the results. These state that projected sales are now 25% higher than the original forecast.

Change the order of the slides so that Slide 4 becomes Slide 5. Save the presentation as **GIFTS4**. Print the speaker's notes.

Check your documents with the examples given at the back of the book.

Consolidation 2

Document 1

Using the following reference sheet, set up a presentation as instructed.

Instructions for master slide style		
Component	**Input**	**Additional information**
Background	One used consistently throughout presentation	Ensure legibility of text against background on printout
Company name	SPORTS & LEISURE	Font: Default
Date	Today's date	Font: Default
Your name	Insert your name	Font: Default
Slide numbering	Insert slide numbers	Font: Default
Company logo	Suitable graphic from Clip Art	

Instructions for text styles				
Style	**Font**	**Size**	**Emphasis**	**Alignment**
Heading	Sans-serif	40–52	Bold	Centre
Bullet	Sans-serif	28–38	Default	Left
Sub-bullet	Sans-serif	20–24	Shadow	Left

Design a master slide from the instructions given. Using the master slide, produce four slides from the information given below retaining capitalisation as shown throughout. Save the presentation as **SPORT1**. Print one slide per page and an outline view.

Slide number	Style	Text/graphic
1	Heading Bullet Bullet Bullet Bullet	OVER-50 FITNESS PROGRAMME Every weekday morning 9.30–11.30 am Price includes sport, swimming and toning exercises Personal trainers on hand to help Increases your fitness, stamina and strength
2	Heading Insert	A FITTER NATION Insert bar chart here. See below for data to be used
3	Heading Bullet Bullet	CLUBS AND SOCIETIES Badminton Swimming

	Bullet Bullet Bullet	Squash Netball Bowls
4	Heading Insert	OUR STAFF Insert the chart here. See below for content of chart to be created

Data for bar chart

	2001	2000	1999	1998
Swimming	580	520	470	450
Badminton	140	110	110	80
Squash	320	290	280	240

Use axis labels of **Year** and **Average Weekly Bookings**.

Chart for Slide 4

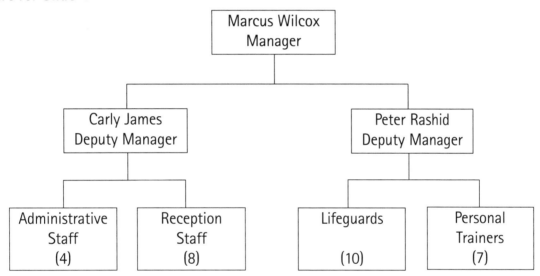

Document 2

Recall the presentation saved as **SPORT1**. Change the bullet symbol style on the master slide and amend the slides as shown below. Save as **SPORT2**. Print all slides as audience handouts (three slides per page). Also print the amended Slide 4 on one full page.

Slide number	Current text	Amendment
1	Every weekday morning, 9.30 am–11.30 am	Delete: 9.30 am–11.30 am
3	Bowls	Add new bullet: Five-a-side Football
4	In the personal trainers box	Amend (7) to (9)

Document 3

Recall the presentation saved as **SPORT2**. Create two further slides from the information given below, retaining capitalisation as shown throughout. Save as **SPORT3**. Print only Slides 5 and 6 together on one page.

Slide number	Style	Text/graphic
5	Heading	CLASSES
	Bullet	We provide classes in the following
	Sub-bullet	Swimming
	Sub-bullet	Aerobics
	Sub-bullet	Aqua Aerobics
	Bullet	Classes run for 10 weeks
	Bullet	Day and evening sessions available
	Bullet	Ask Reception for further details
6	Heading	CRECHE
	Picture	Import a suitable Clip Art picture
	Bullet	For children 6 months–4 years
	Bullet	Open 9.00 am–5.30 pm
	Bullet	1-hour sessions available
	Bullet	Reservations not always necessary

Document 4

Recall the presentation saved as **SPORT3**. Delete the slide containing the organisation chart. Enter the following text as speaker's notes, retaining capitalisation as shown throughout. Ensure the headings on the notes are emphasised with bold. Please check the spelling of the circled words.

Slide 1	Slide 2
OVER-50 FITNESS PROGRAMME	A FITTER NATION
Our specially designed programme for the over 50s is extremely popular. Personal trainers supervise the sessions and ensure you (exercise) at the correct pace.	We are pleased to report that we do seem to be becoming a healthier nation. The bar chart shows the increase in weekly bookings for the three main activities at the sports (center).

Slide 1 (cont'd)	Slide 2 (cont'd)
You will increase your level of fitness, and build stamina and strength — (essential) for a healthy body.	It is hoped that we will be able to attract more users at the Centre in the coming year.

Slide 3	Slide 4
CLUBS AND SOCIETIES The sports and leisure centre is home to many local clubs and societies. At (present) there are clubs for the sports shown. Joining a club is great fun. You will meet people whilst (increaseing) your fitness levels. If you would like to find out more, please ask at reception for details.	CLASSES We (currantly) offer classes in swimming, aerobics and aqua aerobics. We hope to increase the range of classes over the next few months. Our swimming classes are extremely popular and are held on a variety of days and times. There are classes for both adults and children. The aerobics classes are very popular with all ages. These are held every evening between 5·30 and 6·30 pm. Wear loose clothing + trainers. Aqua aerobics combines the best of both worlds. Places on this course are limited and so it is (advisible) to book in advance.

Slide 5
CRECHE We are very proud of our creche which is available for children aged 6 months to 4 years. It is fully supervized by trained staff. The creche is open each weekday from 9.00 am until 5.30 pm. Sessions last for 1 hour and cost £3.50. Reservations are not always necesary.

Change the order of the slides so that Slide 2 becomes Slide 1. Save this document as **SPORT4**. Print the speaker's notes.

Check your documents with the examples given at the back of the book.

Part 6

This part tells you exactly what the examiner will be looking for when marking your work. It does this by showing you the most common errors made in presentations submitted for the examination, together with hints on how to resolve these errors.

It also includes two examination practice exercises for you to complete to prepare you for the OCR examination itself.

Document 1

This document requires you to set up a master slide and a basic presentation. You must print the slides – one per page – and an outline view of all.

What is the examiner looking for?

The examiner is looking for the following:

- All the items on the master slide have been included.
- The text styles are exactly as requested.
- The footer items are present and correct.
- The slides contain the correct information.
- There are no spelling or typographical errors.
- The capitalisation of the text is as shown on the examination paper.
- The images and text do not touch or overlap.
- Items are in the correct position.
- The work has been printed as requested.

Common errors

Look at the slides shown in Figures 6.1 and 6.2 which relate to the January Courses presentation which you worked through. Can you find any errors?

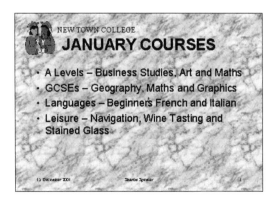

Figure 6.1 Correct version

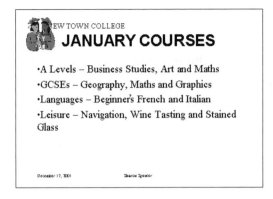

Figure 6.2 Incorrect version

There are six errors in Figure 6.2. Did you spot them?

Error 1

The company name – in this case NEW TOWN COLLEGE is touching the image. *Solution*: Move the text placeholder over slightly so that the text does not touch the image. (See page 6 for details on how to do this.)

Error 2

There is no space between the bullet and the text. *Solution*: Adjust the space between the bullet and the text on the bullet style contained within the master slide, otherwise all the slides in the presentation will contain this error. (See page 20 for instructions on this.)

Error 3

The text is in a serif font rather than sans-serif as instructed. *Solution*: Correct the text styles on the master slide. Remember you must change the master slide, otherwise this will not be changed on all the slides in the presentation. (See page 14 for instructions.)

Error 4

The date is displayed in American format – that is the month before the day. This is not acceptable in OCR examinations. *Solution*: You will need to change to an English display – the day before the month. To do this, go to the **Date and Time** option on the **Insert** menu. Make sure that the **Language** is set to English (UK).

Error 5

The slide number is missing. *Solution*: Ensure that you have activated the slide number check box that is contained in the Header and Footer box. (See page 8 for further information.)

Error 6

The background is missing. *Solution*: Check that you have set a background. If not, see page 5 for information on how to set backgrounds. If you have, check that the Grayscale and Pure Black and White check boxes are not ticked on the print menu. (See page 30 for further information.)

Look at the slides given in Figures 6.3 and 6.4 to see if you can find any errors.

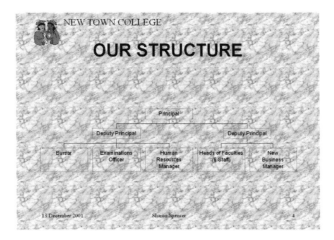

Figure 6.3 Correct version

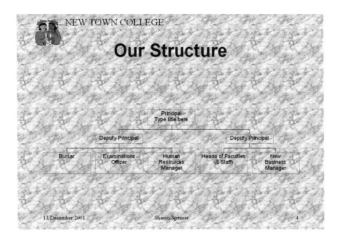

Figure 6.4 Incorrect version

There are two errors in Figure 6.4.

Error 1

The capitalisation of the heading ('Our Structure') is not as specified on the reference sheet. *Solution*: Change the case to that given on the reference sheet.

Error 2

The box 'Principal' contains the words 'Type Title Here'. This would incur 1 fault. *Solution*: Go back into the organisation chart and delete the words. (See page 27 for further information.)

Other errors

It is extremely important that all the elements contained on the master slide are present and correct. If you set the master slide correctly then you should not have many problems with the other slides. Given below are other common errors found in Document 1.

Error – heading not as specified. *Solution*: Ensure you read the instructions very carefully and use the correct capitalisation. When you have completed the slide, check your work.

Error – text styles incorrect. *Solution*: Go back to the master slide and check that the text styles have been set correctly. If you have altered text manually on each slide, then you will need to go to the master slide and change the styles there.

Error – slides not printed. *Solution*: You must ensure that all the slides are printed for this task. Ensure that **All** is checked on the print box. (See page 31 for further information on printing.)

Error – Outline view not printed or incorrect. An outline view containing all slides in your presentation must accompany the printed slides. (Check the instructions on page 31.)

Document 2

This document requires you to amend the slides by adding more text, replacing text, adding sub-bullets and text, amending the organisation chart and changing the style of the bullet points.

What is the examiner looking for?

The examiner is looking for the following:

- All the items on the master slide are still present.
- The text styles are exactly as requested.
- The slides contain the correct information.
- The amendments have been made as specified.
- The bullet style has been changed, but not the text style of the bullet.
- There are no spelling or typographical errors.
- The capitalisation of the text is as shown on the examination paper.
- The images and text do not touch or overlap.
- Items are in the correct position.
- The work has been printed as requested.

Common errors

Look at the slides from the College presentation shown in Figures 6.5 and 6.6. There are a number of errors – can you find them?

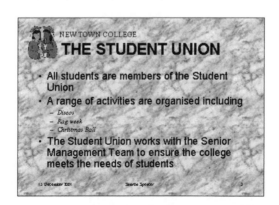

Figure 6.5   Correct version

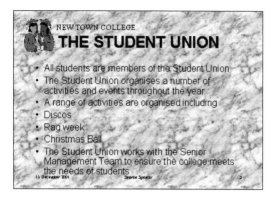

Figure 6.6 Incorrect version

There are four errors in Figure 6.6.

Error 1

The bullet style has not been amended as specified. *Solution*: The bullet point must be changed to something recognisably different from the original. (See page 35 for instructions on how to change bullet points.)

Error 2

The sub-bullets are incorrect. The sub-bullet should be indented from the original bullet and should be styled as stated on the reference sheet. *Solution*: Set the sub-bullet style on the master slide. (See page 36 for further information.) If this has been set correctly, then you must ensure that the sub-bullet is indented once the text has been keyed in. Use the **Promote** button to do this – instructions are given on page 36.

Error 3

The amendment to text is not as specified. The text should have been replaced and not added. *Solution*: Read the instructions very carefully and remember to check your work. If you are short of space, resize the placeholder. (See page 37 for details.)

Error 4

The text has changed size. *Solution*: This is probably because the placeholder is too small to fit all the text at the correct size. If this happens check that you have in fact amended the text correctly (the example in Figure 6.6 has extra text). If you have, then alter the size of the placeholder – see page 37 for details. The text should change automatically to the correct size. If it does not, then you will need to change it manually.

Other errors

Error – names on organisation chart cannot be seen. *Solution*: The boxes on the chart may have a dark fill. Remove the fill altogether or replace with a very light fill colour. (See page 29 for further information.)

Error – text added in an incorrect position. *Solution*: Check your slide very carefully with the instructions given on the examination paper.

Error – audience notes are incorrect. *Solution*: Read the instructions carefully to ensure that you have the correct number of slides (and space for notes) to a page. Ensure you have completed the various options on the Print menu correctly. (See page 39 for details.)

Document 3

This document requires you to create two further slides, one containing a graph and the other a piece of Clip Art.

What is the examiner looking for?

The examiner is looking for the following:

- All the items on the master slide are still present.
- The text styles are exactly as requested.
- The slides contain the correct information.
- Two new slides are created as specified.
- There are no spelling or typographical errors.
- The chart contains titles, axis labels, legends and values as specified.
- The Clip Art is placed correctly.
- The capitalisation of the text is as shown on the examination paper.
- The images and text do not touch or overlap.
- Items are in the correct position.
- The work has been printed as requested.

Common errors

Look at the slides from the College presentation shown in Figures 6.7 and 6.8. There are a number of errors – can you find them?

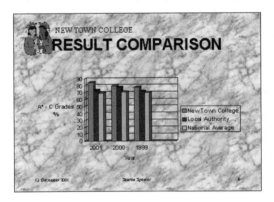

Figure 6.7 Correct version

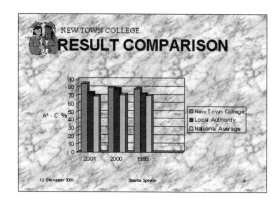

Figure 6.8   Incorrect version

There are two errors in Figure 6.8.

Error 1

The category X axis has the label **Year** missing. *Solution*: Go back into the chart and, using the **Chart Type** sub-menu, key in the label. (See page 48 for details on how to do this.)

Error 2

The category Y axis is incomplete. There is a word missing. *Solution*: Go back into the chart and, using the **Chart Type** sub-menu, amend the label. Read the examination instructions very carefully.

Look at the two slides shown in Figures 6.9 and 6.10.

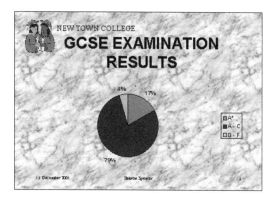

Figure 6.9   Correct version

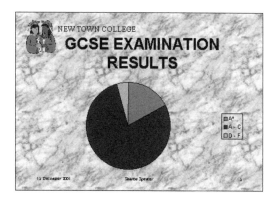

Figure 6.10   Incorrect version

There is one error in Figure 6.10.

Error

The percentages are not shown. This would incur a penalty. *Solution*: Go back into the chart and choose: **Chart Types**. On the tab marked 'Labels' choose 'show percent'. (See page 46 for further information.)

Other errors

Error – the legend on a pie chart is not displayed in full. *Solution*: Double-click on the chart so that the handles appear. Double-click on the legend to display the handles. Resize the box until all text is displayed in full. Click off the chart to return to Normal view. Check that the text is now displayed fully.

Document 4

This document asks you to change the order of the slides and to key in speaker's notes.

What is the examiner looking for?

The examiner is looking for the following:

- All the items on the master slide are still present.
- The text styles are exactly as requested.
- The slides contain the correct information.
- There are no spelling or typographical errors contained in the notes.
- The capitalisation of the text is as shown on the examination paper.
- The images and text do not touch or overlap.
- Items are in the correct position.
- The slides are in the order requested.
- The work has been printed as requested.

Common errors

Error 1

There are spelling and typographical errors in the text. *Solution*: Proofread your work carefully to ensure that all the text has been included. When you are absolutely sure that all the text has been keyed in, then use the spellcheck facility to correct any errors. Pay particular attention to ensuring that the headings on the speaker's notes match exactly the capitalisation and style (i.e. bold, italic etc.) of the heading on the slide. If you have time at the end of the examination, check each slide again to see if any errors have been missed.

Error 2

The speaker's notes have not printed. *Solution*: Check that you have changed the options in the Print menu correctly. (See page 59 for further information.)

Error 3

The slide order is incorrect. *Solution*: You must remember that when you change the order of the slides, PowerPoint automatically renumbers the slides. Therefore, if you are asked to move Slides 4 and 5, for example, the minute you move Slide 4, the slides are no longer in the original order and have been renumbered. Make sure you know the titles of the slides that are to be moved. Do not rely on Outline view to check they are in the correct position. Go to Slide Sorter view to ensure they are correct. (See page 58 for further information.)

Examination Practice 1

Complete the following presentation within 1½ hours. (Worked examples of these documents can be found at the back of the book.)

Document 1

Design a master slide from the instructions on the reference sheet on page 85. Using this master, produce four slides from the information given below, retaining capitalisation as shown throughout. Save the presentation as **FASHION1**. Print one slide per page and an outline view.

Slide number	Style	Text/graphic
1	Heading	COMPANY HISTORY
	Bullet	Founded in 1987 by Jacques Pascal
	Bullet	Jacques studied at London School of Fashion
	Bullet	First collection shown in 1988
	Bullet	Awarded Designer of the Year 1989, 1994, 1998
	Bullet	Team of 6 designers work on 4 collections per annum
2	Heading	WHO'S WHO
	Insert	Insert organisation chart here – see below for content of chart to be created
3	Heading	COMPANY AIMS
	Bullet	To create innovative high-fashion designs for women
	Bullet	To produce garments of the highest possible quality
	Bullet	To be recognised as a leading fashion house
	Bullet	To encourage and assist young designers
4	Heading	OUTLETS
	Bullet	Branches in London, Paris and Milan
	Bullet	Carefully selected department stores
	Bullet	Leading fashion stores throughout the UK

Organisation chart for Slide 2

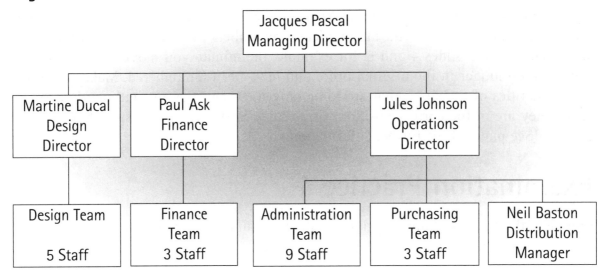

Document 2

Recall the presentation saved as **FASHION1** in Document 1. Change the bullet symbol style on the master slide and amend the slides as shown below. Save as **FASHION2**. Print all slides as audience handouts (three slides per page). Also print the amended Slide 2 on one full page.

Slide number	Current text	Amendment
1	Team of 6 designers work on 4 collections per annum	Replace with: The design team create 4 exciting collections each year
2	Add a further subordinate to Jules Johnson, Operations Manager	Add: Richard Bowman Manufacturing Manager
2	In the Administration Team Box: 9 Staff	Replace with: Administration Team 7 Staff
4	Leading fashion stores throughout the UK	Add sub-bullet: Poppy's – Manchester Add sub-bullet: Fashion UK – Edinburgh Add sub-bullet: Style – Leeds

Document 3

Recall the presentation saved as **FASHION2**. Create two further slides from the information given below retaining capitalisation as shown. The bar chart should display a legend and axis labels. Save as **FASHION3**. Print only Slides 5 and 6 together on one page.

Slide number	Style	Text/graphic
5	Heading	2001 FIGURES
	Bar chart	Refer to table below for data. Use labels of Year and £000's
6	Heading	FUTURE PLANS
	Bullet	New branches in Rome and Zurich
	Bullet	Increase profit margin 4%
	Bullet	Open new manufacturing centre
	Picture	Insert a suitable Clip Art picture

Data for bar chart

	2001	2000	1999	1998
Sales	28.1	27.4	25.6	20.4
Overheads	26.3	24.3	22.4	18.6

Document 4

Recall the presentation save as **FASHION3**. Delete the slide containing the bar chart. Enter the following text as speaker's notes. Ensure the headings on the notes are emphasised with bold and that capitalisation is followed. Please check the spelling of the circled words.

Slide 1	Slide 2
COMPANY HISTORY Jacques Pascal studied at the London School of Fashion winning the coveted Collection of the Year prize in 1986. Upon leaving he decided to produce his own Collection and with that in mind founded the Company in 1987. The (responce) from the public was extremely (encoraging) and this success was compounded when Jacques was awarded the Designer of the Year prize in 1989. This success has continued with the	WHO'S WHO The chart shows the key (personnal) at Pascal. The design team is led by Martine Ducal who also won the Collection of the Year prize from London School of Fashion. She has played a crucial part in ensuring the designs are always creative and innovative.

Slide 1 (cont'd)	Slide 2 (cont'd)
award being given to Jacques in 1994 and 1998. Jacques now works with a creative and innovative design team. They work hard to create four exciting collections each year.	

Slide 3	Slide 4
COMPANY AIMS The company strives to stay ahead in the competitive world of fashion. We are known for our (commitment) to quality as well as our creative designs. The garments are produced from the very best fabrics available. The detail and finish of our garments ensure our clients remain clients for many years. We are justifiably proud of our in-house training programme for young designers.	OUTLETS At present we have branches in London, Paris and Milan. We also sell through selected London department stores. We have recently selected some (leeding) fashion stores to stock our range and these are located in Manchester, (Edingburgh) and Leeds.

Slide 5

FUTURE PLANS

Our strategy is to open two new branches each year. Next year we will be opening in Rome and New York.

We hope to increase our profit margin over the next two years. This should be achieved by introducing new technology throughout the company and updating our systems.

Our plans to open our own manufactring centre will also help to increase our profit margin.

Change the order of the slides so that Slide 4 becomes Slide 2. Save this document as **FASHION4**. Print the speaker's notes.

REFERENCE SHEET

Follow the design brief, e.g. styles and layout within the ranges shown.

Design brief

Instructions for master slide style

The layout of the master slide text and graphics is not pre-defined but must be consistent across the slide show.

Component	Input	Additional information
Background	One used consistently throughout presentation	Ensure legibility of text against background on printout
Company name	PASCAL	Font: Default
Date	Today's date	Font: Default
Your name	Insert your name	Font: Default
Slide numbering	Insert slide numbers	Font: Default
Company logo	Suitable graphic from Clip Art	

Text Styles				
Style	**Font**	**Size**	**Emphasis**	**Alignment**
Heading	Sans-serif	40–60	Bold	Centre
Bullet	Sans-serif	30–40	Default	Left
Sub-bullet	Serif	22–28	Italic	Left

Examination Practice 2

Complete the following presentation within 1½ hours. (Worked examples of these documents can be found at the back of the book.)

Document 1

Design a master slide from the instructions on the reference sheet on page 90. Using this master, produce four slides from the information given below, retaining capitalisation as shown throughout. Save the presentation as **HOLS1**. Print one slide per page and an outline view.

Slide number	Style	Text/graphic
1	Heading Bullet Bullet Bullet Bullet	BARGAIN BREAKS Two- and three-day breaks in Paris, Rome and Amsterdam Four- and five-star accommodation En-suite facilities for all rooms Travel by Eurostar
2	Heading Bullet Bullet Bullet Bullet	PACKAGE TOURS Two- or three-week holidays in Spain, Greece, Ibiza and Cyprus From only £250 per person Half-price reductions for children under 12 Fly from various locations around the UK
3	Heading Bullet Bullet Bullet Bullet	AMERICAN TOURS Two-centre holidays available Long-weekend breaks in New York or Boston Special New England tours in September and October Florida theme park holiday offers
4	Heading Insert	STAFF DETAILS Insert organisation chart here – see below for content of chart to be created

Organisation chart for Slide 4

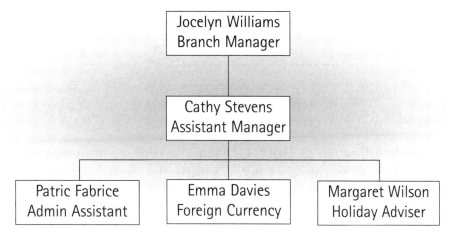

Document 2

Recall the presentation saved as **HOLS1** in Document 1. Change the bullet symbol style on the master slide and amend the slides as shown below. Save as **HOLS2**. Print all slides as audience handouts (three slides per page). Also print the amended Slide 4 on one full page.

Slide number	Current text	Amendment
1	Travel by Eurostar	Add: or fly from Heathrow
2	From only £250 per person	Add: for 14 nights
3	Two-centre holidays available	Add sub-bullet: 1 week at the theme park Add sub-bullet: 1 week relaxing at the coast
3	Long-weekend breaks in New York or Boston	Replace with: Fly-drive touring holidays arranged to your specification
4	Add a further subordinate to Cathy Stevens, Assistant Manager	Add: Ben Craddock Holiday Adviser

Document 3

Recall the presentation saved as **HOLS2**. Create two further slides from the information given below retaining capitalisation as shown. The pie chart should display a legend and percentage labels. Save as **HOLS3**. Print only Slides 5 and 6 together on one page.

Slide number	Current text	Amendment
5	Heading Pie chart	DESTINATIONS 2001 Refer to table below for data. Ensure the percentage labels are displayed
6	Heading Bullet Bullet Bullet Picture	FIND OUT MORE Visit our office – open 7 days a week Call us on 0870 743 55447 Email us at info@toursinc.co.uk Insert a suitable Clip Art picture

Data for pie chart

Greece	Spain	America	Caribbean
4200	3800	2700	1900

Document 4

Recall the presentation saved as **HOLS3**. Delete the slide containing the pie chart. Enter the following text as speaker's notes. Ensure the headings on the notes are emphasised with bold and that capitalisation is followed. Please check the spelling of the circled words.

Slide 1	Slide 2
BARGAIN BREAKS We offer special bargain breaks to Paris, Rome and Amsterdam. These are for three nights, four day stays in luxurious (acomodation). The price quoted is for bed and breakfast. However all hotels offer dining facilities and if you wish, we can book your (restaurent) reservations in advance. Travel is either by Eurostar or you may fly from Heathrow. There is a slight price difference and both modes of travel will be quoted upon request.	**PACKAGE TOURS** These are our most popular holidays and are suitable for families. These represent excellent value for money. Child discounts are available. Your holiday adviser will be able to (advice) you on the most suitable hotels for family holidays. We offer a wide choice of flights to provide maximum convenience to our customers.

Slide 3	Slide 4
AMERICAN TOURS We specialise in American tours and can offer a wide range of holidays to suit the entire family, including Florida theme park trips. Our Autumn in New England tours are superb. You will not (beleive) the spectacular sights of the countryside in full autumnal colour. We provide coach tours so that you can make the most of the (scenary).	**STAFF DETAILS** Our friendly and helpful staff are committed to ensuring you enjoy your holiday to the full. We can advise on the most suitable (locasion) and accommodation for your needs. We can also book activities and tours in advance, so if there is something you would like to do, just ask!

Slide 5
FIND OUT MORE If you would like to (disccuss) your holiday requirements with us in detail, then visit our office. We are open 7 days a week. If more convenient call us on 0870 743 55447 and speak to one of our specially trained advisers. If you (preffer) you can e-mail us with your requirements. We will then contact you by phone or email by return.

Change the order of the slides so that Slide 1 becomes Slide 3. Save this document as **HOLS4**. Print the speaker's notes.

REFERENCE SHEET

Follow the design brief, e.g. styles and layout within the ranges shown.

Design brief

Instructions for master slide style

The layout of the master slide text and graphics is not pre-defined but must be consistent across the slide show.

Component	Input	Additional information
Background	One used consistently throughout presentation	Ensure legibility of text against background on printout
Company name	TOURS INC	Font: Default
Date	Today's date	Font: Default
Your name	Insert your name	Font: Default
Slide numbering	Insert slide numbers	Font: Default
Company logo	Suitable graphic from Clip Art	

Text styles				
Style	**Font**	**Size**	**Emphasis**	**Alignment**
Heading	Sans-serif	38–48	Bold	Centre
Bullet	Sans-serif	28–36	Default	Left
Sub-bullet	Serif	18–24	Italic	Left

Exercise 1.30

Exercise 1.31

1 ⊟ **JANUARY COURSES**

- A Levels – Business Studies, Art and Maths
- GCSEs – Geography, Maths and Graphics
- Languages – Beginner's French and Italian
- Leisure – Navigation, Wine Tasting and Stained Glass

2 ⊟ **MISSION STATEMENT**

- We aim to provide a high standard of education
- Access to new technology will be available to all students
- Our examination results will always be above the national average

3 ⊟ **THE STUDENT UNION**

- All students are members of the Student Union
- The Student Union organises a number of activities and events throughout the year
- The Student Union works with the Senior Management Team to ensure the college meets the needs of students

4 ⊟ **OUR STRUCTURE**

Skills Practice 3

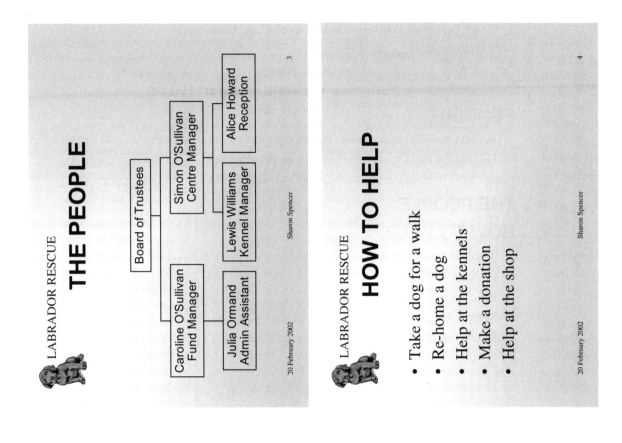

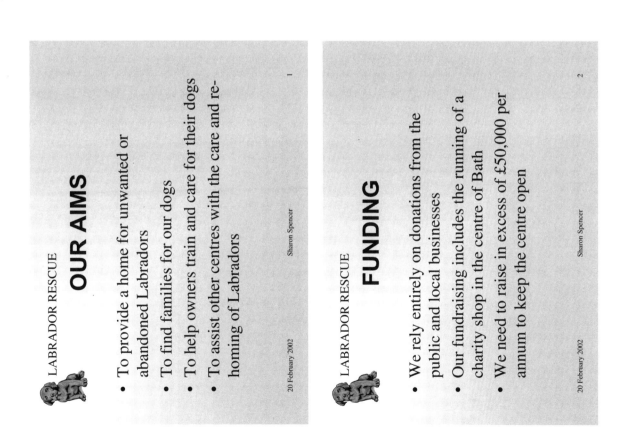

Skills Practice 3 (cont'd)

1 ⊐ OUR AIMS

- To provide a home for unwanted or abandoned Labradors
- To find families for our dogs
- To help owners train and care for their dogs
- To assist other centres with the care and re-homing of Labradors

2 ⊐ FUNDING

- We rely entirely on donations from the public and local businesses
- Our fundraising includes the running of a charity shop in the centre of Bath
- We need to raise in excess of £50,000 per annum to keep the centre open

3 ⊐ THE PEOPLE

4 ⊐ HOW TO HELP

- Take a dog for a walk
- Re-home a dog
- Help at the kennels
- Make a donation
- Help at the shop

Skills Practice 4

Customer Service Policies

AB TRAINING

✓ A carefully considered customer service policy will ensure success

✓ The policy should have clear aims and objectives

✓ Policies should be drawn up after consultation with all staff

✓ Policies should be easy to implement

21 February 2002　　Sharon Spencer

3

Internal and External Customers

AB TRAINING

✓ Internal customers – colleagues

✓ External customers – customers of the business

✓ Both are equally as important when formulating a customer service policy

21 February 2002　　Sharon Spencer

4

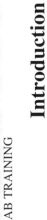

Introduction

AB TRAINING

✓ Customer Service – An Overview

✓ Customer Service Policies

✓ Internal and External Customers

✓ Strategies for dealing with unhappy customers

21 February 2002　　Sharon Spencer

1

Overview

AB TRAINING

✓ Customer Service is the key to business success

✓ Every member of the company is involved

✓ Successful customer service includes internal customers as well as external

21 February 2002　　Sharon Spencer

2

Skills Practice 4 (cont'd)

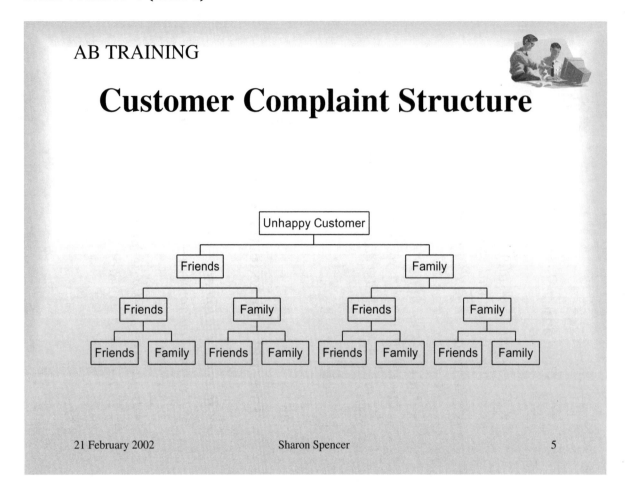

1 ▢ Introduction
- ✓ *Customer Service – An Overview*
- ✓ *Customer Service Policies*
- ✓ *Internal and External Customers*
- ✓ *Strategies for dealing with unhappy customers*

2 ▢ Overview
- ✓ *Customer Service is the key to business success*
- ✓ *Every member of the company is involved*
- ✓ *Successful customer service includes internal customers as well as external*

3 ▢ Customer Service Policies
- ✓ *A carefully considered customer service policy will ensure success*
- ✓ *The policy should have clear aims and objectives*
- ✓ *Policies should be drawn up after consultation with all staff*
- ✓ *Policies should be easy to implement*

4 ▢ Internal and External Customers
- ✓ *Internal customers – colleagues*
- ✓ *External customers – customers of the business*
- ✓ *Both are equally as important when formulating a customer service policy*

5 ▢ Customer Complaint Structure

Exercise 2.7

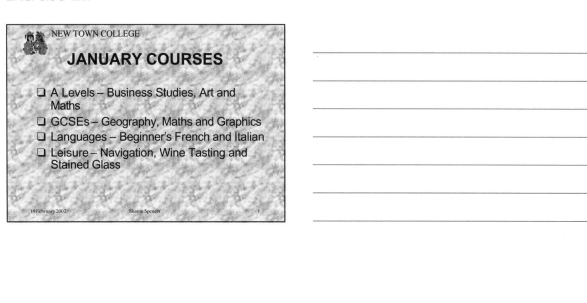

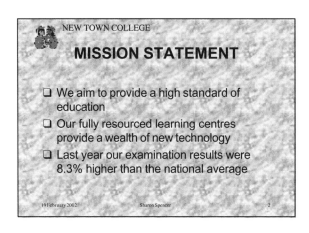

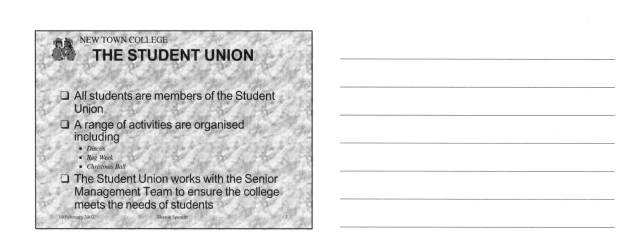

Exercise 2.7 (cont'd)

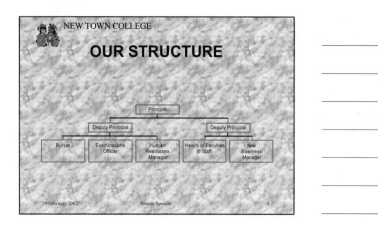

Skills Practice 5

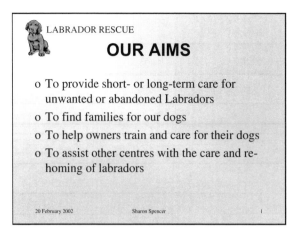

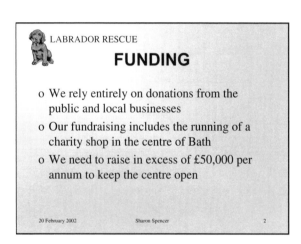

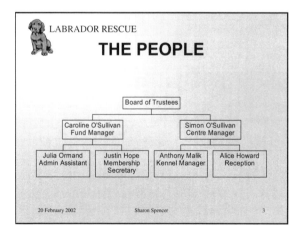

Skills Practice 5 (cont'd)

LABRADOR RESCUE

HOW TO HELP

o Take a dog for a walk
o Re-home a dog
o Help at the kennels
o Make a donation
o Help at the shop
   • By donating unwanted items
   • By serving in the shop
   • By collecting items from others

20 February 2002   Sharon Spencer   4

_____

_____

_____

_____

_____

_____

_____

Skills Practice 6

AB TRAINING

Introduction

- *Customer Service – An Overview*
- *Customer Service Policies*
- *Internal and External Customers*
- *Customer Complaint Structure*
- *Financial Benefits*
- *Strategies for dealing with unhappy customers*

21 February 2002   Sharon Spencer   1

AB TRAINING

Overview

- *Customer Service is the key to business success*
- *Successful customer requires all staff to become involved*
- *Successful customer service includes internal customers as well as external*

21 February 2002   Sharon Spencer   2

AB TRAINING

Customer Service Policies

- *A carefully considered customer service policy will ensure success*
- *The policy should have clear aims and objectives*
- *Policies should be drawn up after consultation with all staff*
- *Policies should be easy to implement*

21 February 2002   Sharon Spencer   3

AB TRAINING

Internal and External Customers

- *Internal customers – colleagues*
- *External customers – customers of the business*
  - Buyers of goods and services
  - Suppliers of goods and services
- *Both are equally important when formulating a customer service policy*

21 February 2002   Sharon Spencer   4

Skills Practice 6 (cont'd)

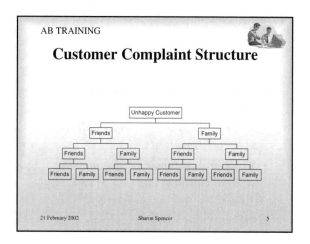

Skills Practice 6 (cont'd)

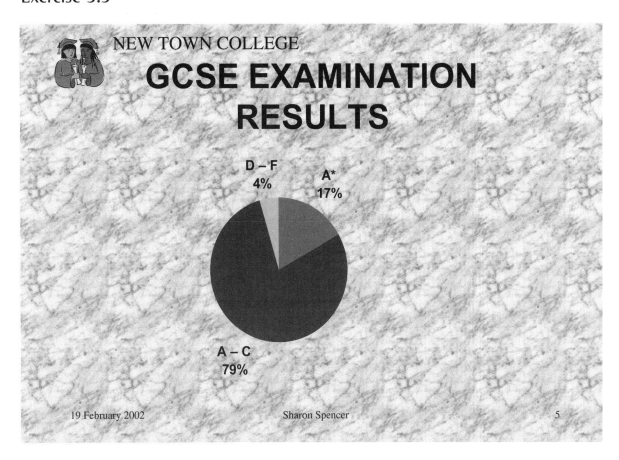

AB TRAINING

Internal and External Customers

- *Internal customers – colleagues*
- *External customers – customers of the business*
  - Buyers of goods and services
  - Suppliers of goods and services
- *Both are equally important when formulating a customer service policy*

21 February 2002　　　　Sharon Spencer　　　　4

Exercise 3.3

NEW TOWN COLLEGE

GCSE EXAMINATION RESULTS

D – F
4%

A*
17%

A – C
79%

19 February 2002　　　　Sharon Spencer　　　　5

Exercise 3.4

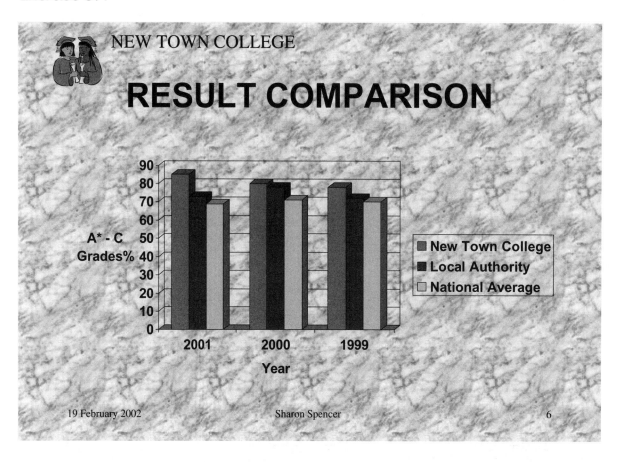

Exercise 3.5

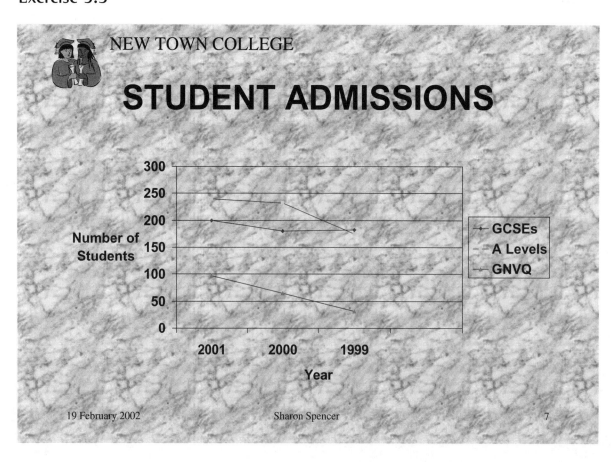

Exercise 3.8

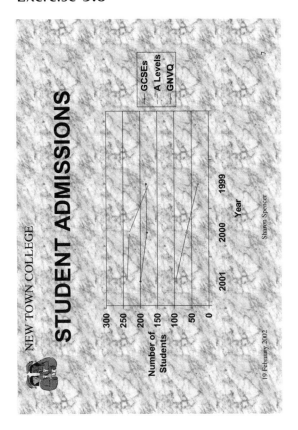

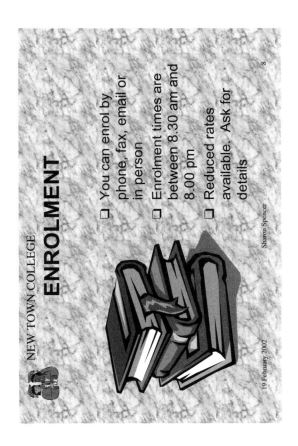

Skills Practice 7

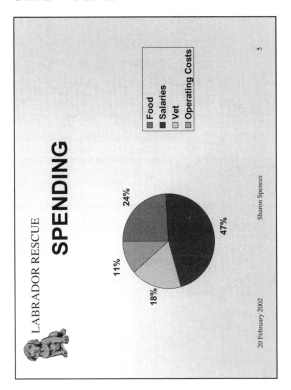

Skills Practice 8

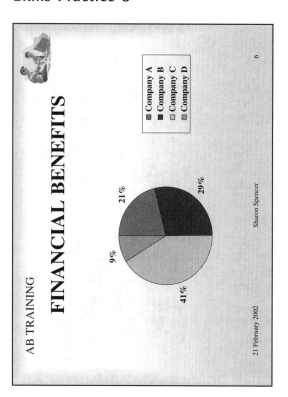

AB TRAINING

FINANCIAL BENEFITS

Company A
Company B
Company C
Company D

21%

9%

41%

29%

21 February 2002

Sharon Spencer

6

AB TRAINING

STRATEGIES

- *Listen carefully*
- *If possible, grant request*
- *If not, state what can be done*
- *Use a polite, friendly and firm tone*

21 February 2002

Sharon Spencer

7

Exercise 4.6

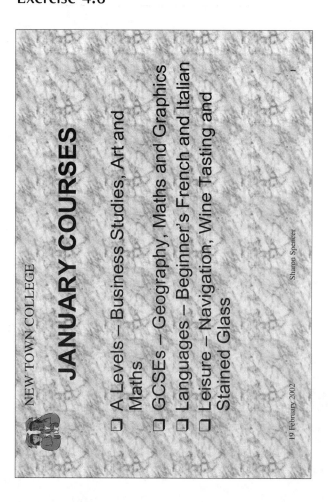

NEW TOWN COLLEGE

JANUARY COURSES

☐ A Levels – Business Studies, Art and Maths
☐ GCSEs – Geography, Maths and Graphics
☐ Languages – Beginner's French and Italian
☐ Leisure – Navigation, Wine Tasting and Stained Glass

19 February 2002

Sharon Spencer

JANUARY COURSES

We offer a range of courses starting in January including A Levels and GCSEs. These will run for five terms with the examinations being taken at the end of the fifth term.

Our language courses are perfect for those hoping to holiday abroad. If you find you enjoy studying a foreign language we offer intermediate and advanced courses beginning in September.

The leisure courses listed here are only a small selection of the wide range on offer. Why not pick up one of our leisure course booklets and choose a new hobby or interest?

Exercise 4.6 (cont'd)

MISSION STATEMENT

We have spent over £50,000 during the past year on updating the three IT centres. Thirty new computers have been purchased and all computers now have Internet access.

Our examination results have been improving year on year and we are now recognised as one of the top performing centres in the local area.

GCSE EXAMINATION RESULTS

The GCSE results were outstanding with the majority of students gaining a minimum of 5 GCSEs at grades A* - C.

We are sure that the excellent results are linked to the progressive teaching methods, well resourced IT Centre and commitment of both staff and students.

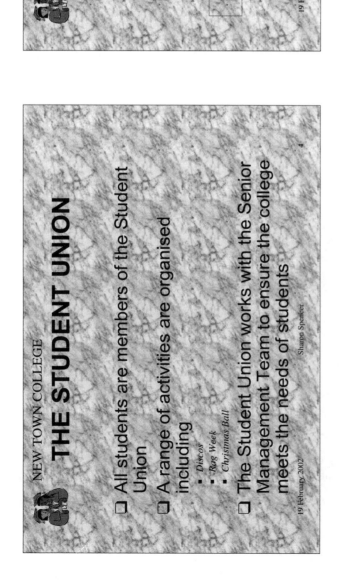

Exercise 4.6 (cont'd)

OUR STRUCTURE

The Senior Management Team meet weekly to discuss college issues.

The Team work together to ensure the college continues to provide the best possible education for its students.

THE STUDENT UNION

The Student Union is thriving at New Town College with many activities and events taking place each term.

Students are encouraged to take part in the wide-ranging activities organised by the Student Union.

Last year the Student Union raised over £10,000 for local and national charities.

Exercise 4.6 (cont'd)

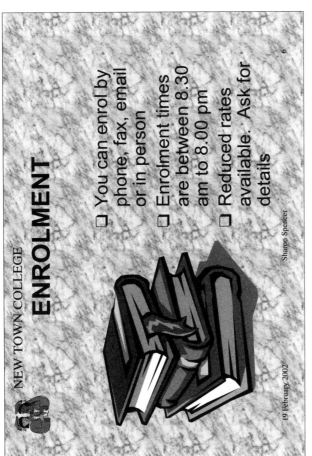

Skills Practice 9

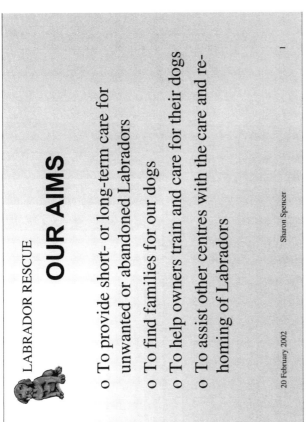

ENROLMENT

We always have helpful and friendly staff on hand to help you enrol on the most suitable course for your needs.

If you would like further advice, please contact the Student Services Officer.

OUR AIMS

We are one of only three centres in the country that specialise in helping unwante Labrador dogs.

We aim to re-home all the animals that are brought into the centre where possible However if this is not possible the dogs stay at the rescue center.

We are keen to promote training classes for owners and their dogs. We help own understand the needs of their dogs and teach the dogs basic obedience skills.

Skills Practice 9 (cont'd)

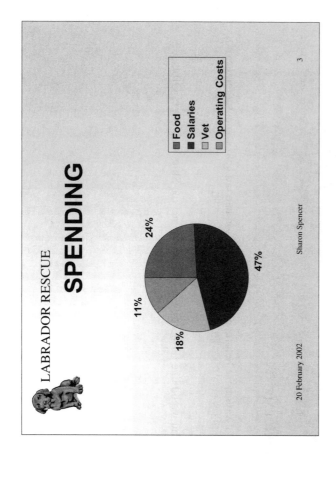

FUNDING

Although we are a registered charity we do not attract any grants from local government. We are however, supported by the local community.

Our recently opened charity shop in the centre of Bath provides a steady income.

The figure of £50,000 increases each year. We need to increase our fundraising activities if our future is to be secure.

SPENDING

Our biggest expense each year is salaries for our staff. However the cost of food for the dogs rose by 9% last year.

The veterinary expenses are low because our local veterinary surgeon charges only minimal fees as a gesture of goodwill. We are very grateful for this assistance.

Skills Practice 9 (cont'd)

EVENTS

The Christmas Sale takes place at the Pavilion on the first Saturday in December each year.

The Centre Open Day takes place on the first Sunday in September.

Training classes are held on Wednesday evenings throughout the year.

The Dog Show, which is held during July attracts visitors from all over the country.

HOW TO HELP

We are always looking for willing volunteers! Dog walkers may take a dog for a walk over the local countryside.

If you would like to re-home a dog our staff will help you to find the most suitable dog.

If you can spare a few hours a week do please help at our shop. If this is not possible then donate items for us to sell.

Make a donation. All donations no matter how small make a significant difference to the Labrador Rescue Centre.

Skills Practice 10

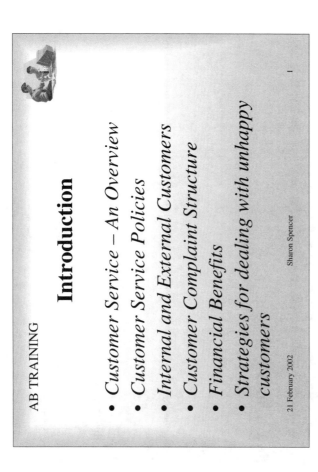

AB TRAINING

Overview

- *Customer Service is the key to business success*
- *Successful customer service requires all staff to become involved*
- *Successful customer service includes internal customers as well as external customers*

21 February 2002   Sharon Spencer

2

AB TRAINING

Introduction

- *Customer Service – An Overview*
- *Customer Service Policies*
- *Internal and External Customers*
- *Customer Complaint Structure*
- *Financial Benefits*
- *Strategies for dealing with unhappy customers*

21 February 2002   Sharon Spencer

1

Overview

Customer Service is the key to business success. Most companies know that repeat business is the most simple and effective way to make profits.

Customer service means so much more than dealing with complaints. A company with an effective customer service policy will rarely have to deal with complaints!

Introduction

Welcome to our Customer Service Training Workshop. I would like to thank you all for coming. The workshop will focus on finding out what exactly is customer service. We will show you how setting a customer service policy can lead to financial benefits and give you some strategies on how to deal with unhappy customers.

Skills Practice 10 (cont'd)

AB TRAINING

Customer Service Policies

- *A carefully considered customer service policy will ensure success*
- *The policy should have clear aims and objectives*
- *Policies should be drawn up after consultation with all staff*
- *Policies should be easy to implement*

21 February 2002   Sharon Spencer

4

Customer Service Policies

Research has shown that every successful business has a carefully considered customer service policy.

The most effective policies are simple and straightforward with clear aims and objectives.

Above all, a policy should be easy to implement. It is important to be realistic about the time and training involved in implementing new policies.

AB TRAINING

Internal and External Customers

- *Internal customers – colleagues*
- *External customers – customers of the business*
  - Buyers of goods and services
  - Suppliers of goods and services
- *Both are equally important when formulating a customer service policy*

21 February 2002   Sharon Spencer

3

Internal and External Customers

The customer service ethos is reflected in the way staff communicate and interact. It is important that customer service is management led and that staff are encouraged to play their part in ensuring the workflow is as efficient and effective as possible.

Do not forget that the suppliers and contractors who deal with your company on a regular basis must also be considered to be customers.

Skills Practice 10 (cont'd)

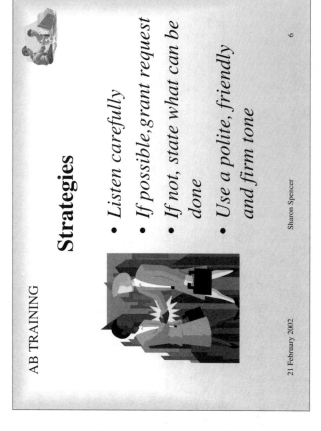

Strategies

One of the easiest and most effective ways of dealing with an unhappy customer is to listen carefully to their complaint.

In most situations the customer already knows what they want the outcome of the complaint to be.

If their solution is unreasonable or unrealistic, say so. However, immediately follow this up with a solution that can be given. Be prepared to negotiate.

Use a polite, friendly and firm tone when dealing with unhappy customers. Appear interested and act with confidence and authority.

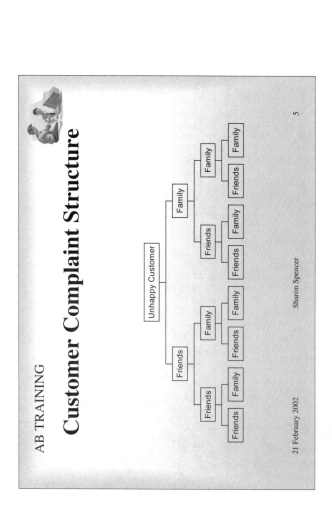

Customer Complaint Structure

This is what happens when a customer is unhappy with the service they have received from your company. They will tell their family and friends. Their family and friends will tell their family and friends and so on.

One very unhappy customer can cost a company hundreds of potential new and satisfied customers.

Unfortunately, a happy customer will not normally tell their family and friends in quite the same way. Why? This is because the customer expects to be satisfied with the transaction they have made with your company.

The chart shows the drastic effect an unhappy customer can have on a company's reputation.

Consolidation 1 – Document 1

CORPORATE GIFTS PLC

ANNUAL FORECAST

- This year's profits will decrease by 14% on last year
- The profit forecast for the next financial year has been reduced to £2 million
- Shareholders' dividends will be reduced by 4% this year

20 February 2002   Sharon Spencer

1

CORPORATE GIFTS PLC

WHAT WENT WRONG?

- Rents, overheads and salaries have increased by over 7% during the last year
- The launch of our new gift range was postponed because of production difficulties
- Nationally consumer confidence has been low

20 February 2002   Sharon Spencer

2

CORPORATE GIFTS PLC

WHAT CAN WE DO?

- Hold current expansion plans
- Consider further reducing shareholders' dividends
- Relocate head office to more economic area

20 February 2002   Sharon Spencer

3

CORPORATE GIFTS PLC

THE FIGURES

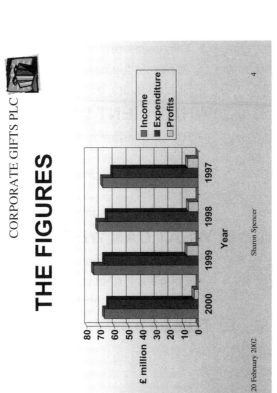

20 February 2002   Sharon Spencer

4

Consolidation 1 – Document 1 (cont'd)

1 ◻ ANNUAL FORECAST

- This year's profits will decrease by 14% on last year
- The profit forecast for the next financial year has been reduced to £2 million
- Shareholders' dividends will be reduced by 4% this year

2 ◻ WHAT WENT WRONG?

- Rents, overheads and salaries have increased by over 7% during the last year
- The launch of our new gift range was postponed because of production difficulties
- Nationally consumer confidence has been low

3 ◻ WHAT CAN WE DO?

- Hold current expansion plans
- Consider further reducing shareholders' dividends
- Relocate head office to more economic area

4 ◻ THE FIGURES

Consolidation 1 – Document 2

CORPORATE GIFTS PLC

ANNUAL FORECAST

- The profit forecast for this year shows a reduction of 14%
- The profit forecast for the next financial year has been reduced to £2 million
- Shareholders' dividends will be reduced by 4% this year

20 February 2002   Sharon Spencer   1

CORPORATE GIFTS PLC

WHAT WENT WRONG?

- Expenditure has increased greatly
  - Rents, overheads and salaries by 7%
  - Production costs by 15%
  - Distribution costs by 10%
- The launch of our new gift range was postponed because of production difficulties
- Nationally consumer confidence has been low

20 February 2002   Sharon Spencer   2

CORPORATE GIFTS PLC

WHAT CAN WE DO?

- Hold current expansion plans
- Consider further reducing shareholders' dividends
- Relocate head office to more economic area and review management structure

20 February 2002   Sharon Spencer   3

Consolidation 1 – Document 2 (cont'd)

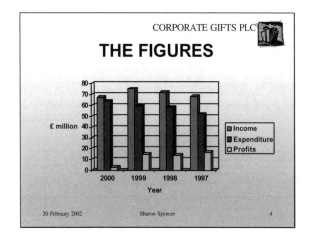

Consolidation 1 – Document 2 (cont'd)

CORPORATE GIFTS PLC

WHAT WENT WRONG?

- ## Expenditure has increased greatly
  - Rents, overheads and salaries by 7%
  - Production costs by 15%
  - Distribution costs by 10%

- ## The launch of our new gift range was postponed because of production difficulties

- ## Nationally consumer confidence has been low

20 February 2002   Sharon Spencer   2

Consolidation 1 – Document 3

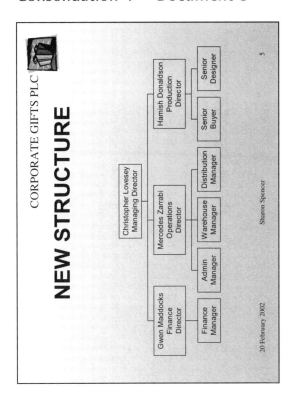

Consolidation 1 – Document 4

CORPORATE GIFTS PLC

WHAT WENT WRONG?

- Expenditure has increased greatly
  - Rents, overheads and salaries by 7%
  - Production costs by 15%
  - Distribution costs by 10%
- The launch of our new gift range was postponed because of production difficulties
- Nationally consumer confidence has been low

20 February 2002

Sharon Spencer

2

WHAT WENT WRONG?

Expenditure has greatly increased during the last twelve months. Inflation has risen and all overheads have increased in line.

The production problems with our new gift range have now been resolved and the launch will take place shortly.

The increase in inflation has affected consumer confidence. We are, however, able to cope with a downturn in business as long as we remain vigilant.

CORPORATE GIFTS PLC

ANNUAL FORECAST

- The profit forecast for this year shows a reduction of 14%
- The profit forecast for the next financial year has been reduced to £2 million
- Shareholders' dividends will be reduced by 4% this year

20 February 2002

Sharon Spencer

1

ANNUAL FORECAST

This year has not matched expectations. The reduction in profits is obviously a matter of some concern.

The forecast of a £2 million profit for next year is the lowest projection. It is hoped that if immediate action is taken this can be increased by an additional £1.5 million.

Our shareholders will be disappointed with their dividend this year, however we are sure that these will increase rapidly over the next few years.

Consolidation 1 – Document 4 (cont'd)

CORPORATE GIFTS PLC

NEW RANGE

- Production difficulties now resolved
- Due to launch within next eight weeks
- Projected sales 25% higher than original forecast

20 February 2002   Sharon Spencer   4

CORPORATE GIFTS PLC

WHAT CAN WE DO?

- Hold current expansion plans
- Consider further reducing shareholders' dividends
- Relocate head office to more economic area and review management structure

20 February 2002   Sharon Spencer   3

NEW RANGE

The production difficulties we have had with the new range have now been resolved. Although we were disappointed with the setbacks we were given the opportunity to undertake more market research and extra publicity. We have been delighted with the results. These state that projected sales are now 25% higher than the original forecast.

WHAT CAN WE DO?

By halting our expansion plans we can ensure that we remain financially secure. This will help us through any recession.

By relocating the head office and reviewing the management structure we are confident that overheads could be reduced by as much as 5% over the next two years.

Consolidation 1 – Document 4 (cont'd)

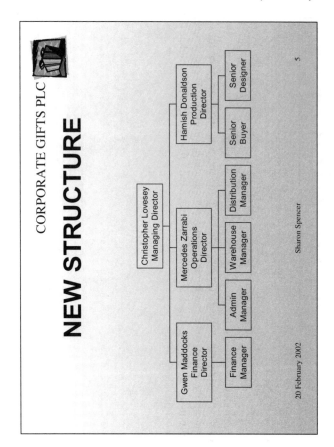

NEW STRUCTURE

This chart shows the proposed new structure for head office. It is a much leaner structure with a level of management removed. Obviously this will lead to staff redundancies but it is hoped that these can be kept to a minimum.

The new structure is only in its first draft. Much will depend on the results of the new product launch and whether we decide to relocate head office.

Consolidation 2 – Document 1

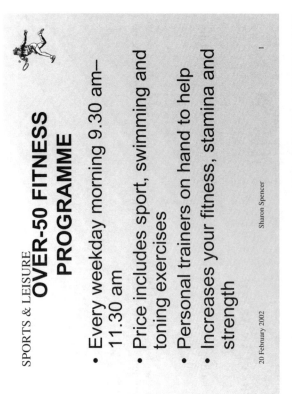

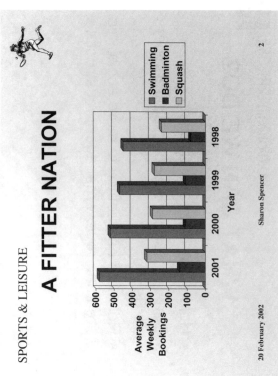

Consolidation 2 – Document 1 (cont'd)

1. OVER-50 FITNESS PROGRAMME
- Every weekday morning 9.30 am–11.30 am
- Price includes sport, swimming and toning exercises
- Personal trainers on hand to help
- Increases your fitness, stamina and strength

2. A FITTER NATION

3. CLUBS AND SOCIETIES
- Badminton
- Swimming
- Squash
- Netball
- Bowls

4. OUR STAFF

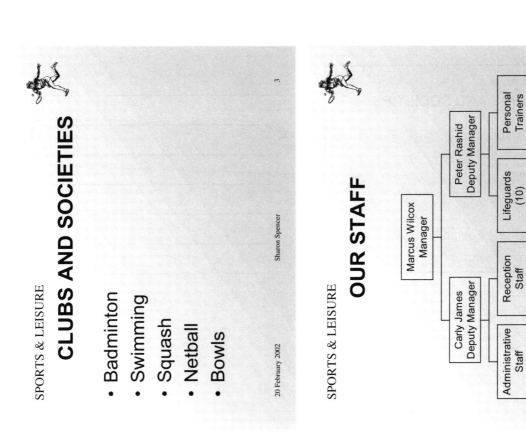

SPORTS & LEISURE

CLUBS AND SOCIETIES

- Badminton
- Swimming
- Squash
- Netball
- Bowls

20 February 2002   Sharon Spencer

3

SPORTS & LEISURE

OUR STAFF

Marcus Wilcox Manager

Carly James Deputy Manager | Peter Rashid Deputy Manager

Administrative Staff (4) | Reception Staff (8) | Lifeguards (10) | Personal Trainers (7)

20 February 2002   Sharon Spencer

4

Consolidation 2 – Document 2

SPORTS & LEISURE
OVER-50 FITNESS PROGRAMME

➢ Every weekday morning
➢ Price includes sport, swimming and toning exercises
➢ Personal trainers on hand to help
➢ Increases your fitness, stamina and strength

20 February 2002   Sharon Spencer   1

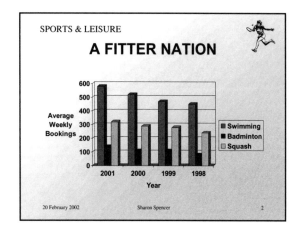

SPORTS & LEISURE
A FITTER NATION

20 February 2002   Sharon Spencer   2

SPORTS & LEISURE
CLUBS AND SOCIETIES

➢ Badminton
➢ Swimming
➢ Squash
➢ Netball
➢ Bowls
➢ Five-a-side Football

20 February 2002   Sharon Spencer   3

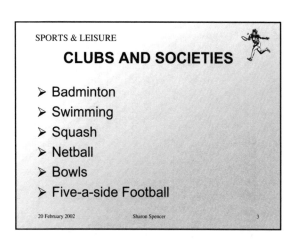

Consolidation 2 – Document 2 (cont'd)

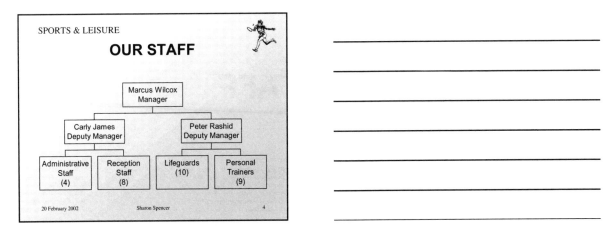

Consolidation 2 – Document 2 (cont'd)

SPORTS & LEISURE

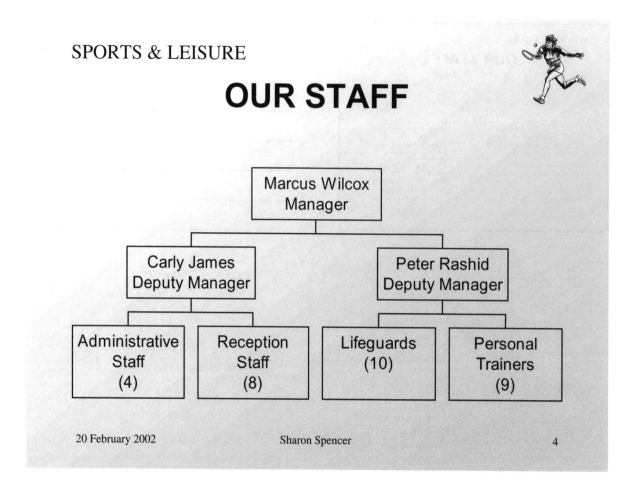

OUR STAFF

Marcus Wilcox — Manager

Carly James — Deputy Manager

Peter Rashid — Deputy Manager

Administrative Staff (4)

Reception Staff (8)

Lifeguards (10)

Personal Trainers (9)

20 February 2002 — Sharon Spencer — 4

Consolidation 2 – Document 3

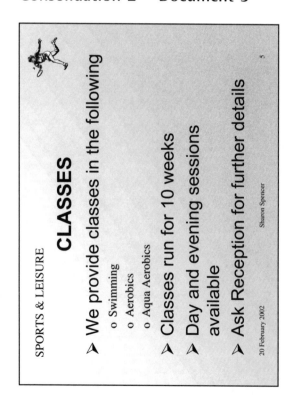

SPORTS & LEISURE

CLASSES

∧ We provide classes in the following

o Swimming
o Aerobics
o Aqua Aerobics

∧ Classes run for 10 weeks

∧ Day and evening sessions available

∧ Ask Reception for further details

20 February 2002 — Sharon Spencer — 5

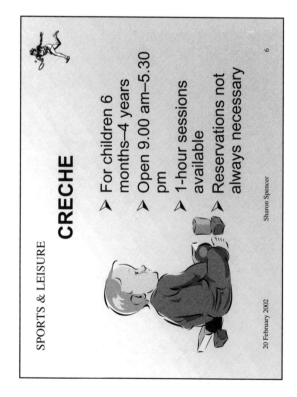

SPORTS & LEISURE

CRECHE

∧ For children 6 months–4 years

∧ Open 9.00 am–5.30 pm

∧ 1-hour sessions available

∧ Reservations not always necessary

20 February 2002 — Sharon Spencer — 6

Consolidation 2 – Document 4

SPORTS & LEISURE

OVER-50 FITNESS PROGRAMME

➤ Every weekday morning

➤ Price includes sport, swimming and toning exercises

➤ Personal trainers on hand to help

➤ Increases your fitness, stamina and strength

20 February 2002

Sharon Spencer

2

OVER-50 FITNESS PROGRAMME

Our specially designed programme for the over 50s is extremely popular. Personal trainers supervise the sessions and ensure you exercise at the correct pace.

You will increase your levels of fitness, and build stamina and strength – essential for a healthy body.

SPORTS & LEISURE

A FITTER NATION

Average Weekly Bookings

Year

- Swimming
- Badminton
- Squash

20 February 2002

Sharon Spencer

1

A FITTER NATION

We are pleased to report that we do seem to be becoming a healthier nation. The bar chart shows the increase in weekly bookings for the three main activities at the sports centre.

It is hoped that we will be able to attract more users at the centre in the coming year.

Consolidation 2 – Document 4 (cont'd)

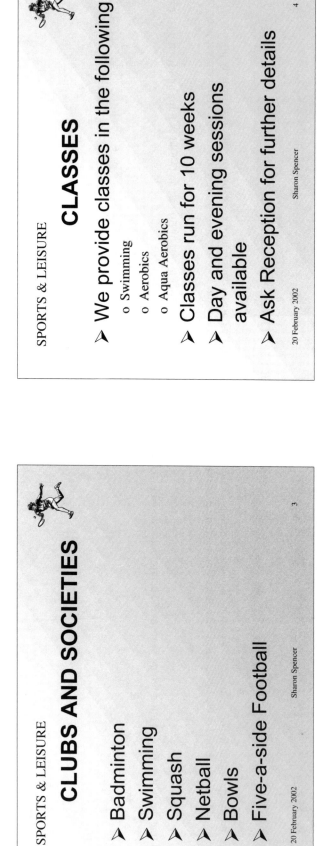

SPORTS & LEISURE

CLASSES

➤ We provide classes in the following
- o Swimming
- o Aerobics
- o Aqua Aerobics

➤ Classes run for 10 weeks

➤ Day and evening sessions available

➤ Ask Reception for further details

20 February 2002   Sharon Spencer   4

SPORTS & LEISURE

CLUBS AND SOCIETIES

➤ Badminton

➤ Swimming

➤ Squash

➤ Netball

➤ Bowls

➤ Five-a-side Football

20 February 2002   Sharon Spencer   3

CLASSES

We currently offer classes in swimming, aerobics and aqua aerobics. We hope to increase the range of classes over the next few months.

Our swimming classes are extremely popular and are held on a variety of days and times. There are classes for both adults and children.

The aerobics classes are very popular with all ages. These are held every evening between 5.30 pm and 6.30 pm. Wear loose clothing and trainers.

Aqua aerobics combine the best of both worlds. Places on this course are limited and so it is advisable to book in advance.

CLUBS AND SOCIETIES

The sports and leisure centre is home to many local clubs and societies. At present there are clubs for the sports shown.

Joining a club is great fun. You will meet people whilst increasing your fitness levels.

If you would like to find out more, please ask at reception for details.

Consolidation 2 – Document 4 (cont'd)

SPORTS & LEISURE

CRECHE

➤ For children 6 months–4 years

➤ Open 9.00 am–5.30 pm

➤ 1-hour sessions available

➤ Reservations not always necessary

20 February 2002

Sharon Spencer

5

RECHE

e are very proud of our creche which is available for children aged 6 months to 4 ars. It is fully supervised by trained staff.

e creche is open each weekday from 9.00 am until 5.30 pm. Sessions last for 1 ur and cost £3.50. Reservations are not always necessary.

Examination Practice 1 – Document 1

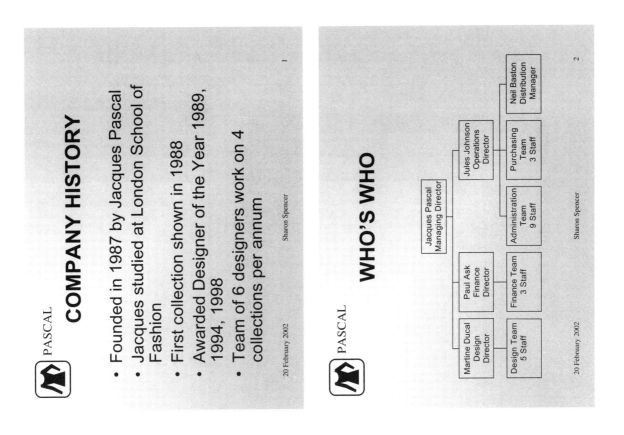

PASCAL

COMPANY HISTORY

• Founded in 1987 by Jacques Pascal
• Jacques studied at London School of Fashion
• First collection shown in 1988
• Awarded Designer of the Year 1989, 1994, 1998
• Team of 6 designers work on 4 collections per annum

20 February 2002

Sharon Spencer

1

PASCAL

WHO'S WHO

Jacques Pascal
Managing Director

Martine Ducal
Design Director

Design Team
5 Staff

Paul Ask
Finance Director

Finance Team
3 Staff

Jules Johnson
Operations Director

Administration
Team
9 Staff

Purchasing
Team
3 Staff

Neil Baston
Distribution
Manager

20 February 2002

Sharon Spencer

2

Examination Practice 1 – Document 1 (cont'd)

1. **COMPANY HISTORY**
   - Founded in 1987 by Jacques Pascal
   - Jacques studied at London School of Fashion
   - First collection shown in 1988
   - Awarded Designer of the Year 1989, 1994, 1998
   - Team of 6 designers work on 4 collections per annum

2. **WHO'S WHO**

3. **COMPANY AIMS**
   - To create innovative high-fashion designs for women
   - To produce garments of the highest possible quality
   - To be recognised as a leading fashion house
   - To encourage and assist young designers

4. **OUTLETS**
   - Branches in London, Paris and Milan
   - Carefully selected department stores
   - Leading fashion stores throughout the UK

COMPANY AIMS

- To create innovative high-fashion designs for women
- To produce garments of the highest possible quality
- To be recognised as a leading fashion house
- To encourage and assist young designers

PASCAL

20 February 2002   Sharon Spencer   3

OUTLETS

- Branches in London, Paris and Milan
- Carefully selected department stores
- Leading fashion stores throughout the UK

PASCAL

20 February 2002   Sharon Spencer   4

Examination Practice 1 – Document 2

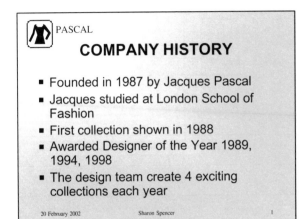

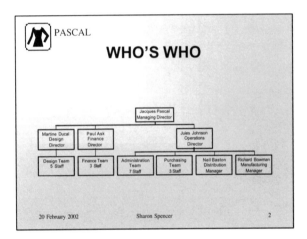

Examination Practice 1 – Document 2 (cont'd)

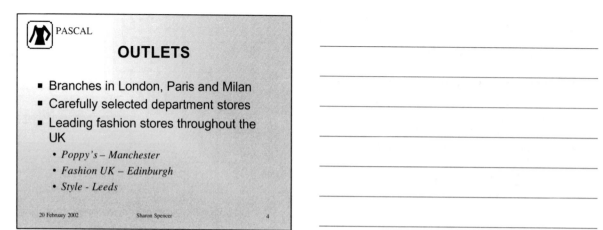

Examination Practice 1 – Document 2 (cont'd)

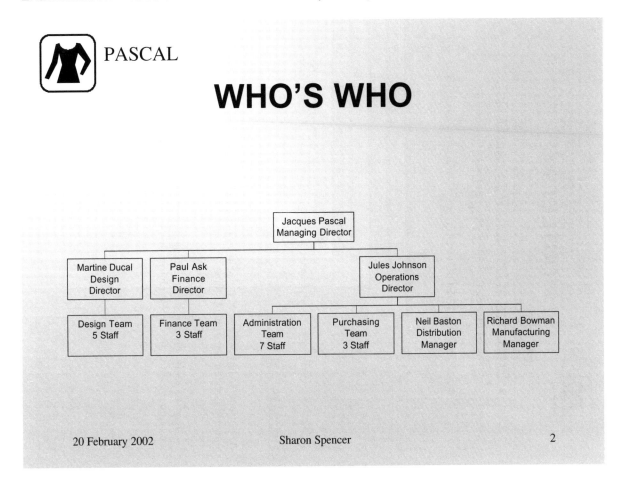

Examination Practice 1 – Document 3

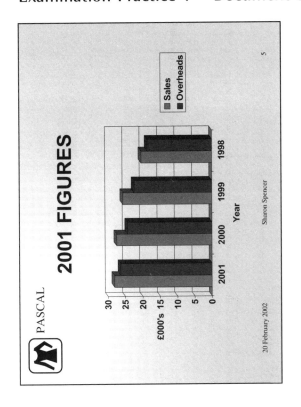

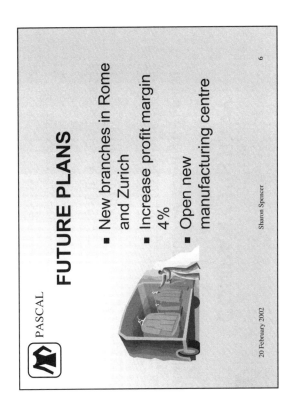

Examination Practice 1 – Document 4

OUTLETS

PASCAL

- Branches in London, Paris and Milan
- Carefully selected department stores
- Leading fashion stores throughout the UK
  - *Poppy's – Manchester*
  - *Fashion UK – Edinburgh*
  - *Style - Leeds*

20 February 2002   Sharon Spencer   2

COMPANY HISTORY

PASCAL

- Founded in 1987 by Jacques Pascal
- Jacques studied at London School of Fashion
- First collection shown in 1988
- Awarded Designer of the Year 1989, 1994, 1998
- The design team create 4 exciting collections each year

20 February 2002   Sharon Spencer   1

OUTLETS

At present we have branches in London, Paris and Milan. We also sell through selected London department stores.

We have recently selected some leading fashion stores to stock our range and these are located in Manchester, Edinburgh and Leeds.

COMPANY HISTORY

Jacques Pascal studied at the London School of Fashion wining the coveted Collection of the Year prize in 1986.

Upon leaving he decided to produce his own collection and with that in mind founded the company in 1987. The response from the public was extremely encouraging and this success was compounded when Jacques was awarded the Designer of the Year prize in 1989. This success has continued with the award being given to Jacques in 1994 and 1998.

Jacques now works with a creative and innovative design team. They work hard to create four exciting collections each year.

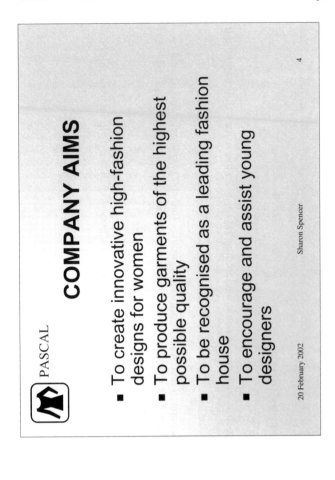

Examination Practice 1 – Document 4 (cont'd)

COMPANY AIMS

The company strives to stay ahead in the competitive world of fashion. We are known for our commitment to quality as well as our creative designs.

The garments are produced from the very best fabrics available. The detail and finish of our garments ensure our clients remain clients for many years.

We are justifiably proud of our in-house training programme for young designers.

WHO'S WHO

The chart shows the key personnel at Pascal.

The design team is led by Martine Ducal who also won the Collection of the Year award from the London School of Fashion. She has played a crucial part in ensuring the designs are always creative and innovative.

Examination Practice 1 – Document 4 (cont'd)

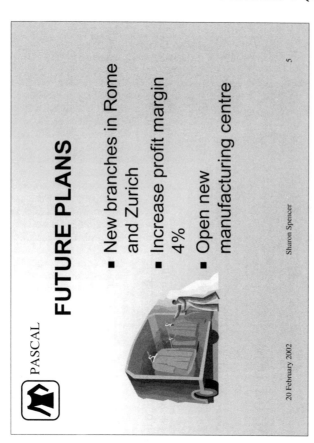

FUTURE PLANS

Our strategy is to open new branches each year. Next year we will be opening in Rome and New York.

We hope to increase our profit margin over the next two years. This should be achieved by introducing new technology throughout the company and updating our systems.

Our plans to open our own manufacturing centre will also help increase our profit margin.

Examination Practice 2 – Document 1

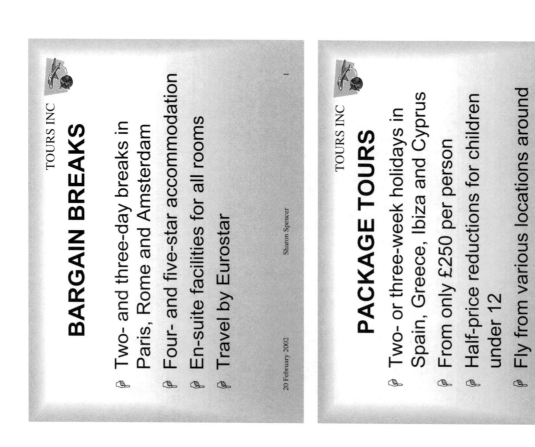

Terminology

Alignment   Positioning of text or graphics on a page in relation to other elements.

Application   This is sometimes used to described the computer software 'program' such as word processing (Word) or database (Access).

AutoLayout   Automatic templates provided by PowerPoint.

Bold   Darker, thicker version of a font or typeface.

Bullets   Symbol that is used to highlight points instead of numbers.

Buttons   Click on a button to select an action – these may appear on toolbars or dialogue boxes.

Character   Letters, numbers and other symbols.

Chart   Graphical display of information, e.g. line, bar, pie or organisation.

Clip Art   Graphic images that are non-copyright.

Clipboard   Where the computer stores items you have copied or cut. They stay on the clipboard until the application is shut down.

Design template   Pre-set templates available in PowerPoint.

Dialogue box   Window (or menu) that is displayed asking you for information.

File   Unit of information stored on the computer – PowerPoint calls files Presentations.

Font   Typeface.

Graphic   Picture, line or drawing.

Handout   Printed pages containing slides and often space to write notes.

Header and Footer   Specified areas at the top and bottom of a page in which information can be displayed on all pages or slides contained in a document.

Indent   Text moved in from the left margin.

Italic   Sloping version of a typeface.

Justification   Another word for alignment, usually used for text that is flush to both margins.

Lower case   Small letters.

Master slide   A slide on which items are placed and the background set so that all slides contained within a presentation have a consistent appearance.

Menu   List of commands grouped into related tasks from which you can choose.

Object   Content on slides and in placeholders – e.g. Clip Art, chart.

Panes   The various parts of a split window – e.g. the outline pane, note pane, etc.

Placeholder   Boxes in which to insert text, charts, graphics, etc.

Point   Unit of measurement for type sizes.

Right click   Click the right-hand mouse button to display further menus.

Sans-serif   Typeface that does not have strokes on the bottom of letters, such as m or n.

Scrollbar   Horizontal or vertical bar that appears at the side or bottom of a window or pane. By clicking on the arrow, the contents will move through a document.

Select   Highlight a piece of text or graphic chart or image so that you can amend or change it.

Serif   Typeface that does have strokes on the bottom of letters.

Slide   Pages created in PowerPoint.

Slide show   A series of related slides that work together to make a presentation in PowerPoint.

Template   A slide with pre-set styles on which you can base your presentation.

Text box   Box in which text is inserted.

Text wrap   Invisible border of space around the graphic image that acts as a barrier between text and graphics.

Typeface   Family of type characters – e.g. Times New Roman or Arial.

Undo   A command that will reverse your most recent action(s).

Upper case   Capital letters.

Word wrap   Automatically starts a new line when text reaches the end of current line.

Keyboard shortcuts

Keyboard	Menu
F1	Help
F5	View slide show
F7	Spellcheck
F12	Save file
Ctrl + A	Selects all items on slide
Ctrl + C	Copies selected item
Ctrl + D	Duplicates the entire contents of a slide
Ctrl + F	Displays the **Find** dialogue box
Ctrl + H	Displays the **Replace** dialogue box
Ctrl + M	Inserts a new slide
Ctrl + N	Opens a new presentation
Ctrl + O	Opens an existing presentation
Ctrl + P	Displays the **Print** dialogue box
Ctrl + S	Saves the presentation
Ctrl + V	Pastes a copied item
Ctrl + X	Cuts selected item from page
Ctrl + Y	Redo a clear (resets an item you have removed using **Undo**)
Ctrl + Z	Undo
Alt + F4	Exits PowerPoint
Esc	Cancels items
Del	Deletes items

Glossary

The menu and mouse actions change depending on what you are doing in PowerPoint. For example, if you click on a text placeholder, then the menus will relate to text manipulation such as alignment, enhancement, spacing, etc. Ensure that you have selected the correct type of item – graphic or text – before you use this guide.

Action	Keyboard	Mouse	Right-mouse menu	Menu
Action buttons, add				Slide Show Action Buttons
Action settings			Action Settings	Slide Show Action Settings
Background format			Background	Format Background
Bold text	Ctrl + B	Click the Bold button	Font Select: Bold	Format – Font Select: Bold
Bullets, change type			Bullets and Numbering	Format Bullets and Numbering
Capitals, change to after keying in				Format Change Case Uppercase
Centre text	Ctrl + E	Click the Center button		Format Alignment Center
Change case				Select text Format Change Case Select case
Chart, insert using AutoLayout		Select appropriate slide, using New Slide button		
Clip Art, insert		Click: Insert Clip Art button		Insert Picture Clip Art
Close a file	Ctrl + W	Click the Close button		File Close
Cut text	Ctrl + X	Click the Cut button	Cut	Edit Cut
Delete an image	Select the image, press: Delete			

Delete a word	Double-click on the word Press: **Delete**			
Delete a slide	Select the slide in the **Outline** view and press the **Cut** button			
Exit PowerPoint	**Alt + F4**	Click the **Close** button ❌		**F**ile E**x**it
Font, change		Click the down arrow next to **Font** box to select new font	**F**ont	F**o**rmat **F**ont
Font size, change		Click the down arrow next to **Font Size** box to select new size	**F**ont	F**o**rmat **F**ont
Headers and footers				**V**iew **H**eader and Footer
Help	**F1**			**H**elp
Insert text	Position cursor in correct place and key in text			
Master Slide view				**V**iew **M**aster **S**lide master
New presentation, create	**Ctrl + N**	Click the **New** button 🗋		
New slide	**Ctrl + M**	Click the **New Slide** button 🔲		**I**nsert **N**ew Slide
Notes, add	In Normal view/Outline View, add to the **Notes** pane			
Number slides				**I**nsert **Slide Number** (and check the box in Header and Footer)
Open and existing file	**Ctrl + O**	Click the **Open** button 📂		**F**ile **O**pen